D0204673

THE
HUMAN
MARKETPLACE

THE
HUMAN
MARKETPLACE:

An Examination of Private Employment Agencies

Tomás Martinez

Transaction Books
New Brunswick, N.J.

Library of Congress Catalog Number:74-20196
ISBN:0-87855-094-1

Printed in the United States of America

Library of Congress Cataloging in Publication Data
Martinez, Tomás, 1942-
The human marketplace.
Bibliography: p.
Includes index.
1. Employment agencies.   I. Title.
HD5861.M37   331.1'28   74-20196
ISBN 0-87855-094-1

Para Mis Profesores

First of all: what is work? Work is of two kinds: first, altering the position of matter at or near the earth's surface relatively to other such matter; second, telling other people to do so. The first kind is unpleasant and ill paid; the second is pleasant and highly paid. The second kind is capable of indefinite extension: there are not only those who give orders, but those who give advice as to what orders should be given. Usually two opposite kinds of advice are given simultaneously by two organized bodies of men; this is called politics. The skill required for this kind of work is not knowledge of the subjects as to which advice is given but knowledge of the art of persuasive speaking and writing . . . .

Bertrand Russell
In Praise of Idleness

PREFACE

Academic research should be done for the pure intellectual joy that is naturally generated when only objective facts are pursued and analyzed.

I call the phenomenon of private employment agencies, "the human marketplace" because my research demonstrates that it is a useful case study for gathering data on the evolution and influences upon the relationship between work and identity.

My professional interest in private employment agencies began during the spring, 1964. My friend and fellow sociology senior at the University of Illinois, Ollie Martin, suggested that a sociology student with an interest in work and identity would undoubtedly learn much about the world of work by taking a summer job as an employment agent. I followed his advice. When I began graduate studies in sociology at the University of California, Davis the following fall, I systematized my field notes for a term paper. Over the next two years, I discussed my participant observation research with students in my section on introductory sociology. I then rewrote the paper and sent it to TRANS-ACTION magazine, which published it. It generated about forty letters that served to increase my interest.

I thought of the title of this book three years before the Office of Manpower Policy, Evaluation and Research of the U.S. Department of Labor awarded me a research grant (No. 91-05-68-72) to collect more information about private employment agencies. It was fun trying to chart the history of private employment agencies, and I was helped by the work of John Hederson, my research assistant, and my colleagues at the University of Santa Clara, Gene Lehr, Les Rosenthal, and Paul Verden.

CONTENTS

INTRODUCTION

The Social Role of Private Employment Agents

Private employment agents—men and women who derive an income by acting as brokers between employers and people who seek employment—are a relatively recent phenomenon in human history. They are an example of a highly specialized division of labor—itself a recent phenomenon. Private employment agents can exist only while labor is a commodity subject to free pricing within a market economy and when the laborer is free to leave his employment or geographic area in pursuit of better wages and/or working conditions. While we tend to take such an environment for granted, it evolved no earlier than the end of the eighteenth century. This is not to suggest the total absence of labor mobility prior to the late 1700s. Labor mobility was, however, understood and dealt with as a political-economic problem and not as a virtue to be encouraged by allowing private men to traffic and profit in it.

Consequently, private employment agents in their pure form cannot be expected to exist prior to the development of a free labor economy, nor, despite exhaustive research, did I find any evidence to the contrary.[1] However, I did find, as might be expected, that the recruiter-broker function of contemporary employment agents was performed increasingly throughout history, but it was one of a cluster of functions fulfilled by a single man, either for a single political employer (rather than a number of private ones) or as a minor part of another role from which he drew an income and an identity.

The social role of private employment agent developed within a social context characterized by four general societal processes: (1) increasingly rational, efficient solutions to labor problems in a rapidly changing econ-

1

omy; (2) expanding opportunities for entrepreneurs; (3) changing social and self-conceptions of workers; and (4) changing legal definitions of the nature of the relationship between workers, employers and job middlemen. These societal processes are the conceptual themes around which this book is written.

The history of the social world can be viewed as a turn toward more rational means of solving recurrent problems. This tendency is especially noticeable in the administration of governments and business. As governments and business firms grew, so did the need for workers. A rational, efficient means to solve the problem of recruitment had to be devised. Did employment agents evolve as a logical means of solving the recruitment problem?

The capitalistic ideology (Weber's "Protestant Ethic") glorifying hard work and opportunism typically finds expression in areas where a small amount of capital will bear healthy profits.[2] People with such an orientation seek an appropriate role. Entrepreneurs typically move from one enterprise to another, in search of more work and profit. As economies expand, so do the number of entrepreneurs. Was the role of private employment agent a logical choice for entrepreneurs to enter? Did entrepreneurs hasten the expansion of the social role of employment agents?

The growing alienation of workers, a problem of central concern to Marx, occurs not only as workers feel out of touch with the products of their toil and sense no control over their work life, but also as they come to sell themselves as commodities.[3] In a free, capitalistic labor market, the individual worker "disposes of his labour-power as his own commodity."[4] Thus, the laborer *sells* himself as a commodity, implying that he *sees* himself worth a certain market value. In this sense, employment agents share the same insight with Marx—a recognition of the social and self-conception of workers based upon their "commodity value." They differ, however, in their subjective reaction to this insight. To Marx, the worker is exploited by a capitalistic system and should seek to overthrow it, whereas private employment agents understand the commodity value of labor as an opportunity to make a profit. Marx did not examine the role of employment agents as either a promoter or manifestation of the alienation process. What was the role of employment agents in the history of worker alienation in Marx's sense?

The legal system defines for society's members certain rights and obligations. Rights of ownership, or property rights, were considered for the greater part of history to include arbitrary treatment of employees. As people obtained more freedom over their lives, they also obtained more freedom in selecting whom they would work for and for how long, depending upon the alternatives available and the conditions of the economy. The imposition of private employment agents into the employer-worker relationship raises certain legal-societal questions. How did the activities of private employment agents conform or conflict with the dominant legal and political philosophies of the times? And, what are the sociological implications?

Analysis of Job Middleman Role

This introduction describes the social role of private employment agents, outlines the major conceptual themes of this book and comments upon the nature of employment and hiring. In the first chapter, the historical development of the role of job middleman in general, and private employment agents in specific, is examined. The early forerunners of private employment agents are uncovered doing business in the marketplace. I use an "occupational regression" perspective in order to understand the history of the employment agent as an occupational role. According to this simple perspective, any given occupational role is studied in its contemporary specialization and its general functions are traced back to an earlier set of activities which are a part of a complexity of roles serving a similar general function. Occupational regression data presented in this chapter are based primarily upon the European and American experience. In America, the socio-economic climate of the nineteenth century provided a fertile condition for the development of private employment agents. We also see how the economics of the human marketplace influence the nature of the relationship between employment agent and applicant.

Chapter 2 briefly presents basic, descriptive information on the different kinds of "abuses" committed by some private employment agents, practices that have shaped strongly the history of the relationship between agent and society. This information acquaints the reader more fully with the kinds of activities that are of concern in more theoretical terms in the following chapter on the social control of private employment agents. It is sometimes useful to appreciate social phenomena in its own terms before the social scientist renders his explanation. Hence, the aim in the second chapter is to present percepts, which are then reconceptualized in terms of the societal reaction to them in the next chapter.

Chapter 3 contains an analysis of the societal reaction to the abuses by private employment agents, which developed into a major social movement to regulate their activities. The historical process by which certain business practices of private employment agents became legally defined as "deviant" and punishable by law is examined. The legal and political history of this movement is central to governmental attempts to regulate business practices in general. It is necessary to understand the sociolegal climate of the nineteenth century when the philosophical and political struggle over governmental regulation of private employment agencies, and private enterprise in general, took place. Many of the court decisions bearing on the regulation of private employment agencies set certain legal precedents for governmental regulation of private enterprise. In addition to attempts toward direct control of private employment agencies, there developed a movement to control them indirectly through establishing free, competitive public employment agencies. A comparison is made between public and private employment agencies in order to ascertain the extent of indirect control.

In chapter 4 are the circumstances that influence private employment agents to seek professional status, how they are seeking it and whether or not they are succeeding. The notion of "pseudoprofessionalization" is used to designate the process by which many status-seeking occupational groups, such as private employment agents, take on the facade of true professionalization. Pseudoprofessionalization is attempted by private employment agents to gain political power and check governmental attempts to regulate their activities. A close inspection of the nature of the private employment agent's work reveals that it is essentially selling, rather than disinterested, professional counseling, with rare exceptions. A brief analysis of the current status of private employment agents in California suggests increasing political power, with the probability of unregulated activities and the potential for unregulated abuse.

Chapter 5 is concerned with a description and an analysis of data from my study of former private employment agency-users. The nature of the relationship between the private employment agent and his applicant is conceptualized as one of "power dependence."[5] From this perspective, a typology of applicants is developed, based upon their degree of dependency upon the agent, as indicated by their stated reasons for using a private employment agency for the first time. The nature of the experience between agent and applicant appears to be influenced primarily by the extent of applicant dependency. In general, the more an applicant is dependent upon the agent, the greater the likelihood that the agent will (1) pay less attention to the applicant's stated job desires and (2) successfully manipulate the applicant's self-esteem.

The last chapter is concerned with relating certain observations learned in the course of the research and exploring the implications of current socioeconomic trends for the future development of private employment agents. One particularly important concern is the growing political power of private employment agencies and the development of "informal controls" by the government to check its power. The role of the private employment agent in an increasingly technological human marketplace deserves the attention of students of society and manpower planners.

The Nature of Employment and Hiring

Before beginning with the body of this study, some comments are in order about the nature of employment and the hiring situation in general.[6] Potential employers and job applicants enter the hiring situation with markedly different views and concerns. For the employer, the problem is one of selecting from among those who are available, the person who is either likely to do the best job at the price the employer is willing to pay or who will do a minimally competent job at a presumably lower price. Simply stated, the employer is willing to pay a person to perform a task of benefit to the employer. The employee's biological and psychological condition are of little interest to the employer, except in so far as they might enhance or reduce his effectiveness on the job.

However, biological and psychological conditions are of profound importance to the job applicant. The fulfillment of biological and psychological needs drives people to seek employment in the first place. While the biological factors are obvious, some of the psychological dimensions are not.

The hiring situation is one of the relatively rare occasions when a person is subjected to a forthright evaluation and comparison with others. As such, it is an opportunity for testing the self-conception of the job-seeker. This test of self-concept is particularly important in modern societies where economic achievement and occupation are considered generally both as an indicator of one's place in the social structure and of one's value as a human being.

Information about one's self derived from the human marketplace—not from the family, ethnicity, religion or territory—is considered primary data by perhaps the overwhelming majority of people in constructing a response to the universal question, "Who am I?"[7] The hiring situation can be considered a profound identity-defining situation. If one is paid what one considers oneself to be worth, then that is what one is actually worth. But, what happens when a middleman, a professional employment agent, intervenes in the hiring process? How does the employment agent affect the self-defining process inherent in the hiring situation?

NOTES

1. We found an unsupported assertion that private employment agents emerged in the fifteenth century in Germany. Anna Y. Reed, *Occupational Placement* (Ithaca, N.Y.: Cornell University Press, 1946).

2. See H.H. Gerth and C. Wright Mills, eds., *From Max Weber: Essays in Sociology* (New York: Oxford University Press, 1946).

3. See Karl Marx, *Capital*, vol. 1 (New York: Modern Library, 1906).

4. Ibid., p. 186.

5. See Richard M. Emerson, "Power Dependence Relations," *The American Sociological Review* 27 (February 1962):32-41.

6. I am especially grateful for the helpful editorial comments of Les Rosenthal in this section.

7. Emile Durkheim was fascinated by the insight that occupational groups, and work life in general, have come to dominate the lives of large segments of society. Work not only usurped traditional moral authority, but has also evolved into a source of life's fulfillment (sui generis). Emile Durkheim, *The Division of Labor in Society* (Glencoe, Ill.: Free Press, 1947). For an empirical study analyzing the "relative strength of occupational, corporate and religious 'communities'," see Harold L. Wilensky and Jack Ladinsky, "From Religious Community to Occupational Group: Structural Assimilation Among Professors, Lawyers, and Engineers," *The American Sociological Review* 32 (August 1967):541-61.

1

FROM MARKETPLACE
TO MARKETPLACE

The Marketplace

Within a relatively primitive economy there is little opportunity for a specialized professional middleman to make a living as an employment agent. The public marketplace acts as an extremely effective device for bringing together prospective employers and seekers of work. Its location is readily known and accessible to all. Other goods are sold there—why not labor? The buyer and the seller have only to meet one another, make their interests known and agree on terms.

In fifth-century Athens, for example, the Colonos, a special part of the Agora, was set aside specifically as a place for unemployed men to congregate and participate in this process.[1] The writers of the New Testament were familiar with this use of the marketplace, as is suggested by the parable of the laborers in the vineyard:

> For the kingdom of heaven is like a householder who went out early in the morning to hire laborers for his vineyard. And having agreed with the laborers for a denarius a day, he sent them into his vineyard.
>
> Going out about the third hour, he saw others standing in the marketplace idle.[2]

The parable continues with the householder returning several times to hire additional idle workers. Interestingly enough, it concludes with him paying the *last* hired—those that worked only a short time—as much as the first

7

hired ("So shall the last be first, and the first last. For many are called, but few are chosen"). Perhaps the good householder understood the demeaning and anxiety-laden nature of standing among a group of rivals awaiting a potential employer.

The nature of the job marketplace was also quite clear to Henri Pirenne, writing about medieval journeymen:

> For the most part (they) lived in alleys in some room rented by the week and owned nothing but the clothes they wore. They went from town to town hiring themselves out to employers. On Monday morning they were to be met with in the squares and in front of the churches, anxiously awaiting for a master to engage them for a week.[3]

As late as 1834 the city fathers of New York proclaimed that a "place be designated in every market where those who wanted work could meet with those who wanted workers."[4] Even today there are specific streetcorners in many American cities where men seeking labor congregate. The locations are informally determined, the language and clothes are different and the employers and employees arrive by automobile. In many ways, these market corners are functionally identical to the Greek Colonos of 2,500 years ago.

The Job Middleman

Although direct contact between employer and potential employee in the open marketplace is effective and persistent, it has limitations. The numbers of workers needed, the distance from workplace to marketplace and, most importantly, the "busy-ness" of the employers, all reduce the utility of direct personal contact between employer and job-seeker in the hiring situation. Men long ago discovered it is often far more convenient to assign or allow the recruitment and selection function to be performed by a third party, or job middleman. We turn, then, to a review of the historical development of the job middleman who performs his duties for commercial profit.

It is common to view industrial development as a change from simple to complex. The single blacksmith with his few *simple* tools can be taken as the forerunner of the *complex* automobile manufacturing firm with its thousands of employees and specialized machinery. However, when we focus on a single contemporary occupation and retrace its history, we find that far from being simple, the occupational forerunners turn out to have a complex of roles. For example, in the case of the blacksmith, the work duties included selling the product manufactured. Thus, a forerunner of the automobile salesman is also the blacksmith. In addition, while the techniques of a specific role become more complex (e.g., curing the sick), other roles develop to simplify the role-complex (e.g., nurses, nurses' aides, X-ray technicians).

"Occupational Regression"

The term "occupational regression" will refer to a way of tracing the development of a given work role. According to this simple perspective, we begin with a definition of a contemporary specialized occupational role and regress to a consideration of earlier elements of a complexity of roles performing a general societal function. In the case of private employment agents, the most recurrent premodern occupations serving the recruitment and selection of workers function are those resembling the modern general contractor and labor contractor.[5] Some of the components of the contemporary specialized occupational role appear earlier in a variety of guises.

Early Examples of Job Middlemen

One of the earliest examples of job middlemen occurs in Ancient Sumer. The job middlemen were actually temple priests who would enroll and dispatch laborers and servants for temporary employment in neighboring areas.[6] During this period Sumerian priests comprised the ruling elite. A primary concern of the governing body was building "public projects." The need for a steady supply of workers coincided with the development of a more efficient means of processing laborers. By converting their temples into employment agencies and the priests into employment agents, the ruling elite in ancient Sumer enacted an administrative solution to the recruitment problem.

Under the Sumerian system, each worker was given a lump of clay indicating his wages and the length of time for the proposed job. When his work was done, the temporary employer would mark the clay lump with his seal. The worker would then return to the temple, where the clay lump receipt was inspected, verified and filed away by one of the scribes.

Available records suggest that rather than being paid directly by the employer, the worker was, in practice, like an employee of a modern temporary employment agency wherein wages are collected by the agency—in this case, the temple. Instead of paying the agent (the temple priest) a fee, the worker received his wages from the agent with the fee already deducted. It is also likely that the worker was not a free laborer in the modern sense, but owed a political-religious obligation or *corvee*. This service duty remained a persistent feature of theocratic institutions throughout the ancient and medieval world. It was taken for granted as a form of in-kind taxation, although it was occasionally supplemented by wages. For the sake of brevity we will skip a few pages of history and turn to medieval Europe.

Medieval Job Middlemen

The social situation of laborers in premodern times is characterized by general servility, subjection and unfree status. Even those ploughmen and harvesters in medieval Europe not bound by feudal ties to a single master were not "free" in the sense that they could not move freely from one employer to another in pursuit of the best price for their labor. Medieval realms were not small sovereign states where residents could fulfill their legal obligations merely by complying with the existing laws of the realm. Whatever laws existed actually covered relatively few contingencies. In fact, the stability of the realm depended upon the accountability of all residents to persons lesser than the ruler. Almost everyone had liegelike ties to a petty noble, a village, a guild, a religious order or a town. Those without such ties were in a very real sense "outlaws." Even beggars were encouraged to form guilds as a way of regulating their activity and making them accountable. Labor mobility at that time must be understood within this context.

Labor mobility was encouraged primarily by those who wanted undeveloped land developed. For example, twelfth-century German nobles wanted their unoccupied marsh and swamplands drained and settled with people who would become both political and economic subjects.[7] They first addressed themselves to neighboring archbishops and nobles, urging them to encourage their "surplus and hungry populations to emigrate." An early account indicates that "recruiting messengers," who acted as job middlemen, promoted the potential prosperity of new lands to induce laborers to migrate to Germany. A typical advertisement of the recruiting messengers is as follows:

> All who were in want of land might come with their families and receive the best of soil, a spacious country rich in crops, abounding in fish and flesh, and of exceeding good pasturage.[8]

When they arrived, of course, they discovered that this land of milk and honey was a swamp, in need of draining before anything else could be done with it. In spite of the risks involved many workers, usually the more dissatisfied and hungry, were inspired to leave their homeland for better living and working conditions. The source of much of this inspiration was the news spread by messengers and recruiters. Germany in the twelfth century provides perhaps the best example of the impact of private employment agents in medieval times. According to *The Cambridge Economic History of Europe from the Decline of the Roman Empire:*

> The attraction of colonists presented greater and greater difficulties as settlement went forward, especially for non-German lords. The demand was for a long time greater than the supply. We may infer this from the very attractive conditions offered to colonists at the start. We have sufficient evidence from the first half of the twelfth century that it was necessary to send agents to recruit emigrants in the various German regions.[9]

Some of these messengers appear to have been retainers sent out on a particular mission. Others were free-lance entrepreneurs known as locators, who have been described as enterprising men who had "slipped in between" the lord and the settling workers.[10] Locators represent an interesting forerunner because they combined recruitment with other functions, such as those associated with a contemporary construction contractor (i.e., supervision of workers and capital to initiate construction). Locators promoted colonization in Germany through recruiting workers and usually accepted responsibility for an undeveloped region "at his own risk."[11] James Westfall Thompson elaborates the business practices of the locator:

> The immediate instrument in the promotion of colonization was a contractor (locator), which may be appropriately translated "promoter" in American parlance. These agents would contract with a large landed proprietor—bishop or baron, abbot or noble—to bring settlers in and establish them upon the grants which they had acquired from the margrave . . . . One "section" in every such rural community (Landgemeinde) was set aside for the parish priest . . . . One-tenth went to the *locator* as his fee.[12]

Almost anyone could become a locator, from knight to peasant. But, as far as their origins were traced, most locators were burgesses who were, more than other persons, disposed to put acquired capital into land.[13]

In the middle of the fourteenth century the Black Death swept through Europe, decimating the population. The dissolution of feudal ties and the acute labor shortage that followed would seem in retrospect a likely occasion for enterprising men to take up a living as employer-paid recruiting agents. To do so, however, was both illegal and perilous. The universal political reaction to labor shortage and rapidly rising wages was a general, massive repression and regulation of both wages and emigration. Wages were frozen at preplague levels. Laborers were forbidden either to leave their local area or to change employers without governmental permission. Moreover, the able-bodied unemployed were required to accept any offer of employment made at preinflated prices. The *English Statute of Laborers* (1349) is a prominent example of the restrictive labor legislation enacted from Norway to Spain. Although such laws proved difficult to enforce and while the opportunities for an employment broker were great, the penalties for "enticing" employees were even greater.

It is useful to see how medieval masters fulfilled the middleman function. Far from being capitalists (who own the means of production and the raw materials they work on) they were, by and large, labor contractors for journeymen with their own tools who worked on materials owned and supplied by merchant entrepreneurs. Raw materials and work were by no means constant but were subject to continual fluctuations. (It was for this reason that journeymen were so called.) When examined from this standpoint, a master can be considered both manager/supervisor and employment broker for (1) *itinerant* skilled workers and (2) a relatively steady crew of unskilled and semiskilled apprentices.[14]

Neither the decay of the guilds (in the face of rapid and uneven industrial changes) nor the dissolution of manorial economies into national economies significantly altered the status of laborers for the better. Instead, the roads swarmed with an enormous population of "free" men—vagabonds, beggars, roaming day-laborers and every variety of thief. Without ties to place or occupation, they were a terrifying menace to the established order. In an attempt to keep them from draining into the swollen towns and cities, strict settlement laws were enacted, but enforcement proved unsuccessful.

Until the mid-seventeenth century, mass poverty and unemployment were seen as by-products of overpopulation. One of the avowed objectives of early colonial advocates was to "relieve the land of its surplus inhabitants,"[15] whether or not they desired to leave. Abbot Smith suggests there was no desire to learn on the part of the inhabitants:

> there is no evidence that as a class the "surplus inhabitants" had any yearnings for a new and perilous existence in the colonies. When a fever of mass migration appeared, as it did among Puritans in the 1630's, it attacked the moderately prosperous and not the hopelessly indigent, though it might in time spread down in the scale for a short distance.[16]

From 1660 onward, *surplus unemployed workers underwent a social redefinition*. They became viewed more as a valuable commodity and less as a dangerous evil. For example, William Petyt writing in the late 1600s succinctly states the typical British view of labor:

People are . . . the *chiefest, most fundamental* and *precious commodity*, out of which may be derived all sorts of manufacturers, navigation, riches, conquests and solid dominion. *This capital material* being of itself raw and indigested is committed into the hands of the supreme authority in whose prudence and disposition it is to improve, manage and fashion it to more or less advantage.[17]

The idea of a free labor market (with the laborer free to pursue the best price the market afforded) was a "monstrous evil." Not until Adam Smith, writing in 1776, did a respectable writer consider high wages and a free labor market anything other than destructive to the "Wealth of Nations."[18]

Under these circumstances, it is not surprising that the earliest references to employment agencies are the rejected proposals for *public* labor exchanges. In 1650, Henry Robinson proposed that Parliament create an "Office of Addresses and Encounters."[19] Ten years later, a Quaker named Lawson published an *Appeal to the Parliament concerning the Poor that there be no beggar in England* as a "platforme," in which he suggested, "the establishment of Labor Exchanges in the modern sense of the public employment agency."[20]

The proposals were rejected, apparently because they ran directly counter to the prevailing thrust to settle the unemployed in local parishes and "set them on work" on regulated wages as determined by the "supreme authority."[21]

Anglo-American Employment Agents

William Weedon, writing of the period 1640-62 in New England, notes an early attempt to establish a private employment agency in Salem:

A curious effort at civilization, astray and ahead of its proper time, appears in the petition of Ralph Fogg to the General Court for the privilege of an intelligence office or (labor) exchange at Salem. It was not granted.[22]

Weedon does not tell us why the court decided not to allow Mr. Fogg to set up an employment agency, but it is not difficult to make a logical inference. There were, at the time, numerous complaints about high wages extorted by insolent servants (a generic term for all employees). It was probably believed by the court that the establishment of an "intelligence" office would only stimulate the market in "free labor." Moreover, since servants were in demand, the burden of paying the agent's fee must fall on the employer, who may find himself paying fees every time his workers leave.

It was deemed far better to import servants and bind them to labor for a fixed period of time. Indeed, this practice became the major device for importing employees into North America throughout the colonial period. Fully 50 percent of *all* the immigrants during this time arrived as indentured servants. The practice is worth examining in some detail because it appears as the earliest instance of men deriving an income solely by serving as employment brokers or agents of free men.[23]

The indenture contract is the bastard child of the medieval apprentice contract. Basically, a free man binds himself to "be employed in the lawfull and reasonable workes and labors" assigned by his master for a fixed period of time (usually four years) in exchange for food, clothing and the payment of the servant's transportation costs to the New World.[24]

Frequently, the contract called for the granting of a parcel of land or the payment of a lump sum in wages at the completion of the term of service. Skilled workers could bargain for and receive annual wages and/or an exemption from common labor in the fields. The bond servant was by no means a slave, but the contract was rigorously policed and enforced.

Planters were rarely in a position to make the journey to England and thereby select their servants personally. Friends and relatives still in England sometimes acted as direct agents in response to letters, but professional agents appeared quite early and played a crucial role throughout the period.

Earlier, it was noted that the idle poor were not enthusiastic about their emigration to the New World. Abbot Smith, the author of the definitive work on indentured servants, describes the critical role played by the "immigrant agent" in "pressuring" people to become indentured:

> the lower fringes of society can hardly have been touched at all by the influence of books and pamphlets. Some other encouragement was needed, some pressure far more direct and immediate than printed exhortations, before such people would make the final and irrevocable decision to move. This pressure was supplied by the emmigrant agent, generally called during the seventeenth century in England a "spirit" because of his tendency to use improper methods of persuasion, and known in Germany as a "Newlander," or more venomously "Soul-seller." Such agents were paid by ship captains, merchants, or proprietors, generally at a fixed rate per head for all recruits whom they produced ready for transportation.[25]

It was reported in 1638 that the Providence Company agreed with "diverse men" who would "take up" servants for a fixed fee of 20 shillings for each servant. This suggests not only established dealings with agents at that time but also an established negative image of such persons.[26] A hundred years later, a man named James Smith received a request from a group of enterprising Aberdeen merchants to "freight a ship with servants and send it to the plantations."[27] Smith apparently found the task not impossible and rewarding financially, as he used his initiative to literally "drum up" applicants:

> (Smith) hired a drummer to go twice through the town of Aberdeen, announcing the voyage, and sent pipers about at the fair for the same purpose. As the servants came in he superintended their board and lodging.[28]

In general, many of those who followed the drums and pipes of agents like Smith were runaway apprentices who were deceived rather than forcibly kidnapped:

> Alas poor Sheep, they ne're considered where they were going, it was enough for them to be freed from seven years of Apprenticeship, under the Tyranny of a rigid Master . . . and not weighing . . . the slavery they must undergo for five years, amongst Brutes in foreign parts, little inferior to that which they suffer who are Galley-slaves. There was little discourse amongst them, but of the pleasantness of the Soyl of that Continent we were designed for, (out of a design to make us swallow their gilded Pills of Ruine), & the temperature of the Air, the plenty of Fowl and Fish of all sorts; the little labour that is performed or expected having so little trouble in it, that it rather may be accounted a pastime than anything of punishment; and then to sweeten us the farther, they insisted on the pliant loving natures of the Women there; all which they used as baits to catch us silly Gudgeons . . . .[29]

The offices where inticing conversations between agents and recruited workers took place were "Cookes Houses," apparently cheap lodging houses given over largely to housing would-be servants. The indenture contracts were often printed forms with blank spaces for the names to be filled in. Sometimes the contract was signed with the agent or "crimp" (as they were also known) who subsequently sold it to a ship captain or merchant who in turn sold it to the planter upon arrival. James Smith, for example, was acting as an agent for a group of merchants and submitted a bill for his expenses. It was also common in the early period to pay an agent a fee of three pounds for recruiting and housing a servant for indenture, bypassing the agent in the contract process. However, real and imagined kidnappings became so widespread that it became a practice to (1) have the servant testify he had signed of his free will and (2) register indentures before a magistrate.[30]

Very little is known of the agents themselves. Some women were accused of being spirits (i.e., kidnappers) as were a "haberdasher," a hostler, a waterman, two victuallers, a seaman, a brewer's assistant and a shoe-maker.[31] During the early 1720s five men accounted for all the servants registered in the London Guildhall.[32] The volume of business they handled indicates they could have spent very little time at their respective occupations of yeoman, victualler, tobacconist, vinteer and woolcomber.

It was an unsavory and disreputable occupation, apparently profitable and of inestimable importance in the early development of the nation. It diminished in importance toward the end of the colonial period as the supply of free labor increased.

Nineteenth-Century Employment Agents

The early history of private employment agencies—"intelligence offices," as they were first known—remains scattered and buried in an unknown number of sources.[33] In 1966, the U.S. Department of Labor stated "such agencies have been in existence in this country for more than three quarters of a century (1890)."[34]

The National Employment Association (the collective voice of the trade) states in one of their pamphlets: "The private employment agency business in this country is as old as the country itself. Boston and New York newspapers of 150 years ago carried agency or 'broker' advertising."[35]

The only monograph on private employment agencies, a master's thesis written in 1928, suggests "they began operations" about 1820.[36] The earliest specific reference available indicates that the Employers and Servants Protestant Agency was "established in March 1819 for the better regulation of Domestic Servants."[37]

In 1846 appeared one of the first newspaper criticisms of the business practices of employment agents. It concerned a "mysterious" individual who traveled about New England in a "long, low, black wagon" enticing young girls to work in mills:

> We were not aware until within a few days, of the *modus operendi* of the Factory powers in this village, of forcing poor girls from their quiet homes, to become their tools, and like the southern slaves, to give up her life and liberty to the heartless tyrants and task-masters. Observing a singular looking, "long, low, black" wagon passing along the street, we made inquiries respecting it, and were informed that it was what we term "a slaver." She makes regular trips to the north of the state, cruising around in Vermont and New Hampshire, with a "commander" whose heart must be as black as his craft, who is paid a dollar a head, for all he brings to the market, and more in proportion to the distance—If they bring them from such a distance that they cannot easily get back. This is

done by "hoisting false colors," and representing to the girls, that they can tend more machinery than is possible, and that the work is so very neat, and the wages such, that they can dress in silks and spend half their time in reading.[38]

The above description is particularly useful in demonstrating how the recruitment of workers, even when the methods are scandalous, is given attention in an occasional newspaper article but seldom in history books. The old American folk hero Sam Slater ("the father of American manufacturers"), who ran cotton mills in Massachusetts, also recruited farm girls to work in his mill, which helped this self-made, hard-working man build both his reputation and profits. Many of his workers were recruited through an agent, perhaps similar to the above type, who operated during the same period as Slater.[39]

The first large-scale employment agency system appears in 1863 as a variation of the old indenture servant system. This came in the form of The American Emmigrant Company. It was established in order to secure laborers and skilled workers for a number of American employers.[40] It collected varying amounts of fees from employers and a small registration fee from job-seekers in Europe. It also paid the transportation costs of the workers. Rather than recover traveling expenses by selling an employment contract, it had them deducted from the imported worker's wages.

As we approach the later nineteenth century, more published references to private employment agents appear. This is due primarily to publicized attempts to regulate their behavior and enforce licensing. However, the available evidence points to a rapid growth of agencies prior to attempts to regulate them. Their growth coincided with and contributed to industrial development through more efficient recruitment of workers.

When the New York Times started printing its newspapers in 1851, at least two employment agents were already established and alert enough to test the advertising power of the new medium for one week. They placed ads in the paper, which today carries more employment agency advertising than any other paper in the world. The "archaic" flavor of these first ads, although less than 120 years ago, is seen below:

SITUATIONS WANTED—Employment is speedily obtained at No. 114 Nassau St. (basement) for Clerks, Bookkeepers, Porters, Salesmen, Barkeepers, Men on farms and railroads, Waiters, Coachmen, Ostlers; girls for factories, shops and stores; girls as cooks, chamber-maids, girls for general housework, city and country. Charges moderate. References required.

DOMESTIC SERVANTS—Families requiring carefully selected servants are respectfully solicited to patronize the Employers & Servants

Protestant Agency. No. 148 Grant St. Established March 1819 for the better regulation of Domestic Servants.

COLORED HELP—Wanted, at No. 114 Nassau St. a smart likely Colored Man, from 19 to 24 years of age, to go to Connecticut as a table waiter for a respectable and extensive hotel. Wages liberal. None but a smart man need apply.

Thos. Spink Agent[41]

Agents such as Thos. Spink soon began to specialize and ceased to deal with every variety of laborer, from ostler (stableman) to bookkeeper and chambermaid. The early agencies, including all prior to World War I, solicited mostly two distinct types: the manual laborer and the female domestic. There were some general agencies, but it would be more useful to confine our investigation to the more specialized agencies. The applicants, agents, employers, agency locations, fee rates and "counseling" and placement techniques of each type are quite different, varying in different directions for different reasons—primarily depending upon the job market. After examining each type, we will turn toward a third and more recent type: the white-collar agency.

Manual Labor Agencies

Around the turn of the century, the demand for men to do manual work greatly exceeded the supply. Consequently, and not unexpectedly, private employment agents concentrated on this aspect of the labor market. The manual labor agencies handled primarily men, most of whom were newly arrived immigrants. The employers were factories in the eastern states, the railroads and, during harvest season, farmers.

Until World War I, private employment agencies were thriving in the relative prosperity of the times. Their profits came from filling vacant positions with willing workers. Eager entrepreneurs set themselves up, often with a few assistants, as employment agents ready to supply employers with workers. *The gap between industrial labor needs and individuals seeking jobs was bridged by the private agents, who in many cases were the only mediums of information between employers and workmen.* A typical way in which the agents operated is described in a 1914 article:

To get jobs, workmen walk from one agency to another, reading the bulletins written in crayon upon black painted walls and traveling back and forth until they find a job they want, or which they think they can get.

Upon a blackboard is written: "Wanted—25 Tunnel men—soft dirt—$3.50." Men gather and discuss the sign. "Soft dirt" may mean that they will have to work in mud and water. A few workmen are urged to come into the office for information. The clerk says the fee is $2.50 in advance, to be remitted if the job is misrepresented. A description of the work is given, but before the place is made known $2.50 must be paid. Then the workmen are asked to be at the office at some stated time, a few minutes before train time, and as they get on the train they read on their tickets their destination.

Each man must have a "slip," so called, a receipt from the employment agency showing that he has paid his fee and obtained his information from a certain agency.[43]

Thus, in an industrializing society the "slip" replaces the Sumerian lump of clay as an administrative receipt of the employment middleman.

Coming usually from Europe, the immigrant laborer would be happy to take almost any job in order to get a start in this country, and the job he often took was one which his American counterpart, who had been an immigrant a few years earlier, typically snubbed. In need of money and usually far from fluent in English, the immigrant was predisposed toward accepting any form of apparent help in finding a job. To his aid came the private employment agent.

However, this aid rendered to the immigrant was not without implications for his personal adjustment. The immigrant laborer was a valuable commodity to the private employment agency, in the sense that he was the most vulnerable person to the agent's influence and was placed in a job (manual labor) without a great deal of difficulty. The situation in Chicago around 1908 is described by a sociologist who was studying agencies at that time:

The importance of the employment agency in the industrial or economic adjustment of the immigrant became apparent with the first work undertaken by the recently formed League for the Protection of Immigrants. Ignorant of our language, the country, and the American standard of wages, and compelled by his poverty to accept the first possible work, the immigrant is especially defenseless when he offers himself in the labor market. At no time does he need disinterested guidance and help more than in securing his first work, and yet he is dependent in most cases upon the private employment agent and he becomes, because of his ignorance and necessities, a great temptation to an honest agent and a great opportunity to an unscrupulous one.[44]

In what directions then, were immigrant laborers led by agents who succumbed to temptation?

He (the immigrant man) finds himself much handicapped when he tries to obtain work in the country in which he has been led to believe work is most abundant. In the first place, because of his ignorance of English and consequent inability to give or receive directions he cannot work without an interpreter. Interpreters can be profitably employed only when large groups of immigrants work together. Such groups are employed by the foundries, at the stock yards, in mines, on railroads, carline and building construction, in the harvest fields, in ice and lumber camps, and other similar kinds of work. Much of this work is seasonal and is located at a great distance from the city. A large number of men are needed for a few months or weeks to harvest Dakota crops, to build a railroad in Wyoming or Arkansas, to harvest ice in Minnesota, to pick Michigan berries, and to work in the oyster beds of Maryland. This work is most undesirable. The pay is not good—during the past summer agencies were offering from $1.25 to $2.00, usually $1.40 a day. Board is expensive and poor in quality and the work lasts usually only a very short time. Worse than this, the men must come back to Chicago to get their next work, so return railroad fare must be counted on. Such work, because of its undesirability, can usually be obtained. The American workman does not want it because it places him at the mercy of the contractors and employment agencies and makes of him a homeless wanderer. It is work the immigrant can do and, because in most cases he must have work immediately, he takes it gladly.[45]

The status and inner feelings of the "homeless wanderer" awaited the immigrant who was "at the mercy of the contractors and employment agencies."

Many of the contractors and employment agents felt that the immigrant was only temporarily induced to accept unpopular, seasonal work. In a few years he would learn English sufficiently, as well as the "ins" and "outs" of his new homeland, to obtain better work. Regardless of his training or experience, the immigrant still had to serve in the ranks of the unskilled for the start of his occupational career in the States. The agencies, expending the least amount of energy with the maximum return, naturally sought to place all immigrant applicants in the most easily available work, of which there was little variety. Grace Abbott's study of private employment agencies in Chicago bears this out.[46] She investigated 178 of the 289 licensed agencies in the city, and 110 of her sample specialized in placing immigrants; 56 placed only men, 33 only women and 21 placed both. Her findings are summarized in Table 1.

As listed in the table, "gang" work was either construction work outside Chicago or farm work. The "city jobs" consisted of "tearing down buildings and odd jobs on the railroads or in cleaning buildings."[47] The only kind

TABLE 1
Category of Work Offered Immigrant Men and Women
by Chicago Employment Agencies, 1908

Kind of work	Men Only	Women Only	Men & Women (men)	(women)	Total
"Gang work"	49	—	3	—	52
Restaurant or hotel	2	18	15	17	52
Factory	2	4	6	5	17
"City jobs"	8	—	—	—	8
Housework	—	28	—	—	28
Number of agencies	61	50	24	22	157
Agencies counted twice	5	17	3	1	26
Total	56	33	21	21	131

Source: Grace Abbott, "The Chicago Employment Agency and the Immigrant Workers," *The American Journal of Sociology* 14 (November 1908): 290-93.

of work offered by 68 percent of the agencies dealing with immigrants meant traveling a distance of 100 to 1,000 miles from Chicago; from its very nature it was certain to be work of short duration.

Fees paid by applicants (called "registration fees"), payable in advance in cash, were subject to seasonal fluctuation. When the number of unemployed, job-seeking men went up during the winter and mid-summer, so did the fee rate. The maximum "registration fee" that an employment agent in Chicago was legally allowed to charge was two dollars. However, agents supplying unskilled workers never used the registration system and charged any amount they could for a particular job. Fees were found to be higher when the applicant was unable to speak English.[48] An investigator, presenting himself as a man who collected "gangs," asked an agent what fee was charged to the applicants. He was frankly told, "We charge all we can get."[49]

Because of their peculiar business practices, it was impossible for Abbott to find out precisely what fees were charged by the agents in Chicago. But from what the investigators who worked with her found a general range of fees was ascertained. The median fee for "men only" agencies was $3.00-$5.00, with a range of $13.50. For women, both the median ($1.00-$2.00) and the range ($2.50) were substantially lower.

Abbott also describes the locations and neighborhoods where most of the agencies clustered:

Opposite the Union Station on Canal Street from Adams to Madison and from Canal to Clinton on Madison, there is a succession of employ-

TABLE 2
Locations of Chicago Private Employment Agencies Placing Immigrants, 1908*

	Type of Applicants		
	Men	Men &	
Location	Only	Women	Total
Near Saloons & "Cheap			
Lodging Houses"	14	1	15
Near Saloons Only	9	3	12
In Saloons	2	—	2
In Family Rooms	5	3	8
Steamship & Banking Offices	14	—	14
Elsewhere	12	14	26
Total number of agencies	56	21	77

*Figures are from Abbott, op. cit.

ment agencies, saloons, cheap lodging-houses, lunch-rooms, and cheap or second-hand clothing stores. These three blocks are the seasonal labor exchange of Chicago. At any time of the day and until late at night, groups of foreigners may be seen in front of these agencies, and signs offering work in South Dakota, Ohio, or Wyoming are displayed the year round. Most of the other immigrant agencies are along Milwaukee Avenue or in other neighborhoods where our foreign colonies live.[50]

The "facts of interest" of these locations are summarized in Table 2. The locations of the agencies around Union Station gave immediate access to immigrants who came to Chicago from New York and other places by train. Even though there was a law prohibiting the conduct of employment agency business "in or in connection with any place where intoxicating liquors are sold" 45 percent of the immigrant men's agencies were either located "above, below, or next door to a saloon."[51] The fact that 25 percent of the agencies were managed by steamship agents or foreign banks suggests support for the padrone and contractor system.

In New York City, Sixth Avenue was called "Employment Row" in the early years of this century. It was primarily a low-rent neighborhood, consistent with Abbott's description of employment agency locations in Chicago. When an urban renewal project razed the Sixth Avenue strip, the *New York Times* heralded the end of an era that witnessed an interesting procedural tradition of job-finding:

Job seekers have formed the habit of starting at Forty-second or a little further downtown and walking up the West side of Sixth Avenue to scan cards which the agencies put out to show their employment offers.[52]

Why employment agencies tended to cluster in the low-rent neighbor-hoods was answered by the president of the Broadway Association (em-ployment agency group). He pointed out that agencies must remain in such districts in order to clear a profit and to have a central location convenient to transportation facilities. In addition, he claimed it was for the applicant's convenience to have many agencies within a small area.[53]

The typical labor agency of that era in New York was characterized as having two men in the office and about six "recruiters" in saloons, pool halls and other spots frequented by workers. Recruiters usually dressed as workers and mixed with the men, talking of a "fine job" they had heard of. The recruiters' task was to sway workers to "join" them in applying today for that appealing job.[54]

The manual labor agents controlled the distribution of unskilled male labor, with tacit encouragement from both employers and trade unions.[55] In some ways, agents served to ease the unemployment congestion by shipping large numbers of workers out of the cities to work in mines, farms and other places. During periods of unemployment men flocked to the agencies, waiting around for orders to come in and finding temporary shelter within the agency doors. A vivid picture of this was given by a visitor to an agency in New York City in the winter of 1913-14:

Mr. B. (the employment agent) does not run a lodging-place but he allowed the men to stay over night in his place. One night an inspector called and found men sleeping on the bare floor. Two days later he received a letter that he must take out a license for keeping a lodging-house, and that he must not let lodgers sleep on the floor. The same night at closing time he ordered all the men to leave. But when a policeman standing near and some neighbors called him heartless he allowed the men to stay in. He did not charge the men anything. His place consisted of one-half the ground floor, four rooms, in which on some nights he said 364 men were crowded, standing up all night and so packed that it was impossible to pass through. In the morning a baker brings him bread several days old for which he pays three cents a loaf. He breaks every loaf into four parts, but even so there is not enough for one-tenth of his applicants. The men fight for a piece, soak it in water and devour it ravenously. I went through the place, which is barren of any furniture except a few wooden benches, and counted 107 men in the place, most of them standing as there was no place for them to sit down. On account of the severe weather all the windows were closed, and the foulness of the

air was indeed indescribable. I approached a number of men whose
protruding cheek bones and red and strangely shining eyes plainly
showed their suffering, and spoke to them in their native tongue. In nearly
all cases the men had not had anything to eat for two or three weeks and
were keeping themselves alive on what they could pick up from ash
barrels.[56]

Such agencies played an important part in the lives of the unemployed.
They often became central meeting places where many activities other than
waiting for a job occurred. Sometimes they developed into "disreputable
houses." An inquiry made by Francis A. Kellor into several agencies in New
York (sometime between 1904-14) illustrates this:

One (private employment agency), in the basement of a tenement, was a
saloon and restaurant, where the men smoked, talked, ate, and drank. At
night they were allowed to sleep on some rude benches. Another, which
advertised "Employment for bakers and confectioners," was a bare
room with a bar, one end being filled with tables and chairs where the men
played cards and drank. Some so-called "hotels" often have a combination office and saloon on the ground floor, and the second and third floors
are used for lodgers. A trip through such a house showed men drinking
and playing cards all over the premises, and in some places, where
women were seen, the men around said they "hang about to get the men's
money, and are favored and encouraged by the house." In one of these
there were card and billiard tables at which several young men were
playing and groups were hanging about the windows and at the bar.
Another was in a dark, gloomy basement with a low ceiling, and filled
with wooden benches which at night were transformed into rude bunks.
This place was filled with all kinds of indescribable baggage, and was
dirty and disorderly beyond description. There was no eating-house, but
employees brought in food, such as cold meat, "street bacon," fruit, etc.
Because of the crowded condition, most of the "placing" was done on
the street, and benches were placed along the sidewalk for the crowds that
could not get in. Another agency, with a hairdressing store in the basement below it, consisted of a large bare room, filled with wooden benches
and chairs. Though women were waiting there, the proprietor said he
never did any business with women employers, and advised his callers
not to get any such help in his neighborhood. There is little reason to
doubt that some of these places are nothing more than disreputable
houses, and that the employment agency is the ruse by which patrons are
attracted.[57]

Agencies not connected with saloons appear to have operated differently. The operation was more businesslike:

> They usually occupy from two to four rooms, keep registries, and transact business in a space set apart by a railing from the general waiting-room, or in a separate room. The walls are frequently covered with maps, and the rooms are clean and well supplied with chairs. Occasionally intoxicated employees are seen, and the office is dirty, but the crowd of idle men is orderly and more or less free from the sodden, disreputable "rounder" found in saloon agencies.[58]

We turn now to examine how the female domestic servant agencies compared with the male manual labor agencies.

Female Domestic Agencies

As one might suspect, the domestic servant agencies dealt largely with immigrant women, who, caught up in their collective sexual status of the times, did not have the social mobility of males any more than native American women had the social mobility of their male counterparts. In Abbott's study, only four of 33 agencies placing women offered the alternative of factory work to housework, hotel or restaurant work. Most often the immigrant woman became a domestic servant, a position she usually held until she married.[59] However, there was a steady rise in the quality of homes and pay as she moved from one job to another.

Abbott reports that of the 33 agencies placing women in Chicago, 27 were in either a kitchen or parlor office.[60] It is noted that the proprietors and help of these agencies were usually women. Kellor found in New York that of 313 offices supplying households, 120 were in tenements, 107 in apartments, 39 in residences and 49 in business houses.[61] Similar circumstances were observed by Kellor in Philadelphia: 84 percent were in private houses, 10 percent in apartments and about three percent each in tenement and business houses.[62] A journey into a few of these various settings where agents did business is made possible through Kellor:

> Up several iron steps, along two or three rambling halls, up a few more wooden steps—and here at last was the "intelligence office" (employment agency), in a small three-room apartment. The "office" proper was apparently a bare little kitchen with a red and white cloth. The only visible attendant was a sallow slip of a girl with a red pigtail, with long thin arms and clawlike hands, washing dishes at the sink. When applied to for

information she obligingly went out on the balcony to call her mother who was visiting in the street below, but who was induced to come in to see her clients.

A second was found in a basement salesroom, where second-hand clothing was piled around in dirty, disorderly heaps, with a living-room curtained off at the back. This so-called office was used as a bedroom at night. A third was a combination baggage- and living-room. The proprietor was an expressman and his wife ran the office. Any left-over baggage was piled in the office at night and utilized for beds or chairs, according to its adaptability. A fourth, literally covered with left-over bundles of waiting employees, had a table in one corner, which contained the remains of a meal, a "day-book," and advertising material. Over in another corner two flashily dressed girls were playing the piano and singing popular songs. In a fifth the proprietor was washing, and we discussed "servants" and "places" to the time of a rhythmic "rub, rub," through clouds of steam and soapy vapor, with an occasional flap of a wet cloth for variation. The sixth was the first floor of a little two-story corner house, in a two-room apartment where the husband worked as a carpenter in one room, while the wife conducted the office in the other.[64]

While the above type of agencies handled the bulk of the domestic servants, there were also the so-called "aristocratic" offices located near the most fashionable part of the city, with well-furnished offices. Both the applicants and employers were treated with respect and business courtesies. Many girls obtained their first job through the "wash-tub" agency. Soon after learning English and the ways of American gas ranges, they usually find the agencies of a better class.

Female immigrants developed relationships with employment agencies that were markedly different from that of immigrant men. The male agencies were oriented to serve the employers (even though the applicants paid the fee), whereas the female agencies (which often made the employer pay the fee) were oriented to serve the applicant. Male employment agents sold jobs to the applicants, while the domestic employment agents sold servants to the housekeepers. In each case, the object being sold was scarce and the buyers were plentiful. *Thus, the buyer or the party paying the fee was not given as much service as the more precious marketable commodity.*

The buyers, the "ladies" of society, were greatly irritated by receiving treatment that was personally less respectful than that received by the applicants. As early as 1872, a New York matron sent a letter to the *New York Times* complaining that domestic agencies, typically called "intelligence offices," conspired to place women unfit for employment:

Dear Editor:

I notice in the columns of your paper a note from "Climax" (an intelligence office that advertised in *The Times*) on "Characters of Servants." Can Climax give me the name of that intelligence office where it is a regulation to find employment for no domestic who cannot be vouched for by an employer with satisfactory answers to a list of printed questions, etc., and can also clarify from experience that this regulation is honestly observed? My own observations, as well as that of all my friends has proved that the advertisement is mere humbug. I believe that in the last two years I have had experience, either in my own family or that of immediate friends, of every intelligence office between Bleecker and Thirty-seventh Streets, and with two honorable exceptions, they proved thorough delusions. Several times I saw in these offices servants whom I know had been discharged for theft, intemperance, inefficiency from their last places, and heard the persons in charge of the office testifying to their possessing the opposite valuable qualities. In an office last Winter, one of these reliable agents brought forward for my sister's inspection, a woman who had been taken by the police from my house the week previous in a state of beastly intoxication, and I had called the office to warn them against procuring another place for her. When remonstrated with, the agent replied: "The girl must live and if we don't find her a situation some other office will do so."

In two of these very offices which make a parade of their "printed forms," I have found the printed forms to be false in every particular, and learned afterwards from one of the employers who was supposed to have filled in the form that she had never done so. I know that although in one instance I refused to fill in the form, after discharging an incompetent servant, the girl obtained a place in a few days, with the form filled in. I leave to your imagination by whom.

Will it not be better for the ladies of the City to make a resolve, *and let it be known publicly*, that they will engage no servant without a *personal* reference of at least six months employment in one family? I believe unless we exact something of the sort, as well as a more respectful demeanor from our servants, we must look forward at an early day to giving up house keeping or doing our own work.

—A Perplexed Housekeeper[65]

Any resemblence between the above housekeeper and the good housekeeper in the biblical parable is inconceivable. But, like many reformist attempts to cure a disagreeable practice, support seems to have rallied slowly to the "Perplexed Housekeeper's" call to arms. It was 20 years later, in 1892, that society women in New York formed a cooperative bureau to obtain domestic help. It was called Ladies in Need of Proper Domestic Servants Cooperative.[66] Hoping to correct abuses on both sides, the bureau promised to deal with only homes and servants of merit. The applicants were charged $.75 per placement, and the employers $2.50 per servant or $1.50 if they were $6.00 annual subscribers. All later record of Ladies in Needs, etc., seems lost, but it was not successful at ending the malpractices attacked.

Another typical practice by domestic employment agencies, which was not advantageous to the would-be employer, was described by an anonymous author in the *Atlantic Monthly*. "Miss Anonymous" discovered through observing and participating in the interaction within an agency that agents persuaded (even compelled) applicants to demand high salaries, thereby reaping higher commissions. Some of the information she gleaned is well worth quoting here:

If Dante had asked me to suggest a circle of Hell deeper, blacker, and more completely outside the pale of possible redemption than any he has pictured, and one that reproduced a scene with which most women of today are familiar, I should unhesitantly have selected an intelligence office—that terrible centre of human traffic, where the secrets of all hearts are exposed, and where dignity and truth find no admittance.

Nothing but devotion to an elderly cook-less aunt would have induced me to become an Intelligence-Office seeker; but family feeling turned my steps to the door of degradation, bearing the laconic label "Domestic Agency."

My first glimpse of cosy little tete-a-tetes dotting the bleak apartment here and there led me to think that I was at a feminine tea-party, so eager was the guzz of voices, raised for the most part in cheerful monologues, occasionally punctuated by unenthusiastic replies. To be sure, in glancing at some of the groups, it was a little difficult to separate the sheep from the goats; but in a few minutes my eye grew accustomed to subtle differences of dress, the interviewers being for the most part less modishly attired than the interviewed. I was glad to see that the lady in charge of the establishment was busy with a successful deal in cook-broking, so that I was permitted to sit on the side lines and enjoy what seemed like an incarnation of those questionable shapes of housemaids and domestic helpers invoked by the art of Miss Beatrice Herford.

As Miss Anonymous assumed a "detached expresion," she jotted down "broken bits of conversation" on her shopping list:

Here a harsh Irish voice on the other side of the room grated into my consciousness. "Sure the good cooks do be getting eighteen dollars a week, und how would you be supposin' as I'd go to a family like yours for fifteen? If it was at the beach you was livin', and you offered me sixteen, may be I'd take it an' may be I wouldn't; but it'll take more than fifteen dollars a week to get me to the mountains, so I'll be lookin' farther and farin' better, I'll be thinkin'.''

Becoming fascinated by the resemblance in type between a sheep and a goat who were confronting each other from the edges of inhospitable chairs, I watched two stout red females glaring at each other, and wondered if they themselves knew which was about to engage the other. Presumably war-profits had drawn the invisible line between them, and a few years ago they would have stood side by side and replied, "Yes marm," when both were asked the questions which one of them now had the privilege—granted by suddenly attained wealth—of putting to the other.

Miss Anonymous's reporting was interrupted by the lady in charge speaking to her:

"Can I do anything for you?" in the non-committal tone of one who was not sure whether I were myself a bird or a wildflower. I told a brief but moving tale of my invalid aunt, and her resort to a fireless cooker which had proved only a little less difficult than the cookless fire. The impassive brokeress glanced coldly at the intimate details of my aunt's menage, revealed by my reluctant lifting of the domestic curtain, and then said reprovingly, "Of course, if you haven't a gas-stove as well as a range, you will find it very difficult to get a maid to stay with you; and the price you mention is absolutely unheard of nowadays. You can't get anyone for less than sixteen dollars a week to take such a difficult place."

"Difficult!" I exclaimed. "Surely I told you there was only one person in the family, and two maids to do what in the old days a general housework girl would have done for five dollars a week."

A superior smile flickered over the features of the lady in charge of this Infernal Circle. "I will see if any of my women care to speak to you, but I hardly think they will be interested in less than sixteen dollars a week," she said; and retiring behind the screen, presently emerged, followed by a very dressy person who swept me with a glance which "took me in" completely, from the hole in my veil to my square heels and squarer toes. I had innocently imagined that I was to do the interviewing, but not at all—the inquisitor with the nodding ostrich-plumes put me through the third degree, and her hostile glare told me that I should be saved the embarrassment of telling her that she would not do.

Did my aunt keep a kitchen maid?

"No." (sniffs)

Did the help have a private sitting-room?

"No." (grunts of contempt)

Did the cook go to church every Sunday, and have Sunday and
Thursday afternoons and every evening free for her own engagements?
"No."

Suppressed scorn of me broke into articulate anger, which was con-
tagious, and we both rose, scarlet with mutual dislike. The Colonel's
Lady and Judy O'Grady were sisters under the skin, and the consciousness of this subcutaneous resemblance completed my sense of humiliation.

"I don't think you will suit me at all," I was beginning; but her harsh
laughter interrupted me. "No, nor I don't think you'll suit me either, nor
you won't suit nobody else," she said; and flounced off behind the
screen.

An overheard comment provided the "key" to understanding the high
wages demanded by domestic servants:

> Then the key to the whole degrading business was uttered by an honest
> Irish voice, a voice of the old school of oratory, saying in a stage whisper,
> "Sure, if you don't be tellin' the boss, I'll come to yez for tin dollars a
> week, and I'm a regular six-dollar-a-week cook! She tells me I ought to
> get sixteen, but I ain't worth it, an' I know it now, an' you'll know it
> soon."
> I rose and stood before the desk, and with wasted dignity took my leave
> instead of my cook, as I had once hoped.[67]

One gets the impression that Miss Anonymous's "square heels and
squarer toes" did little to help her control the interaction inside the employment agency. She was the buyer, but in the female domestic servant agency
it was a seller's market.

In the domestic servant market the desire for servants, coming from both
the old and new rich, was greater than the number of available servants. The
female domestic workers, not the jobs, were the scarce commodity. The
domestic employment agent grasped the situation for what it was worth and,
consequently, attempted to make a profit from the most willing and able
party—the employer. Increasing profits often involved coaxing the applicant to require as large a salary as the employer market would tolerate, to the
chagrin of Miss Anonymouses everywhere.

There were striking differences between the operating methods of the
domestic and those of the manual labor agencies. In effect, manual labor
agents were trying to convince men to pay for a dubious job, while domestic
agents were attempting to convince employers to hire servants—of dubious
character—for higher wages. Another peculiar difference is the modus

operandi of the domestic agencies, which required the would-be employer to search the streets, from agency to agency, for suitable workers. A reverse situation existed in manual labor agency transactions, where the applicants had to walk the streets in search of a job. A possible explanation is that both types of agencies were dedicated to serving neither the employers nor the applicants. They were dedicated, instead, to collecting more and higher fees, and tailored their methods accordingly.

Agencies for men (manual labor agencies) were oriented to please the employer rather than the applicant. Recognizing that jobs were scarcer than job-seekers, the employment agent needed to have a good relationship with the employers in order to receive job orders. As a justifiable reason for collecting registration fees, the agent needed an employer to whom he could send his applicants (even though he may send many more persons than he knew would be hired). Many of the larger agencies with branches in several cities were subsidized by railroads. These agents were more oriented toward giving service to their rail benefactors than to their job-seeking applicants. Since employers could often find workers without the uses of a private agency (they would in theory have company recruiters do the bulk of the job) and since there was a large number of agencies to select from, the agents had to make money from their only other alternative source—the applicant.

Assisted Immigration and Emigration

Immigrant labor was the main supply of applicants for both manual labor and domestic agencies. There was a formidable supply of immigrant men to keep agencies busy, but there was a shortage of women domestics. Most of the servants processed through agencies were either foreign born, Negroes from the South or girls from rural areas. In all three cases the agencies played an influential part in bringing the women to the cities where domestic work was in sharp demand.

With characteristic enterprise, employment agents recruited foreigners through several means. One very successful method was through advertisements in foreign-language newspapers, which were published in the United States and sent overseas.[68] (European newspapers outlawed employment agency ads from the United States in their own papers, which is reminiscent of attempts to outlaw foreign recruiters in medieval times.) The contract labor clause of the immigration law prohibited publishing or printing "advertisements in any foreign country for the purpose of inducing aliens to come here upon promises of employment."[69] Nevertheless, large and eye-catching advertisements that were placed in the American-published papers (including papers in Swedish, Hungarian, Jewish and Finnish, among others) were carried in the pockets and purses of girls arriving by boat.

Another important means of recruiting women living in foreign lands also involved circumventing immigration regulations. Since only relatives were allowed to get the girls out of the immigrant stations, the employment agents would ''send emissaries abroad who get acquainted with girls and send them over with the name of the office, or of some friend with whom the office works and who poses as a relative.''[70] There was an assortment of possible persons who served as paid agents to direct foreign girls, and men, to specific agencies, from priests and postmasters to ticket agents and teachers.[71] Kellor clearly conceptualizes the relationship between immigration and domestic agencies:

> But between the householder and the immigrant stands the intelligence office, which is both a blessing and a curse. To understand this demand for immigrants for households, glance at the methods of some of these offices. They cannot begin to meet the demand normally, so they import girls. They have agents who induce the girls to come over here upon the most extravagant promises; they prepay their passage, and they enter into collusion with boardinghouses to supply them with girls. Upon inquiries during the summer (1904) at agencies we were told ''the proprietor is abroad getting a supply of girls for the winter.''[72]

Girls, especially Negroes, were also imported from the South. White agents worked in southern cities and located girls from outlying districts. They arranged to bring them into the cities and transport them to northern employment offices. The fare to northern cities was often paid by the agents, but the girls usually repaid such aid. For example, girls both from abroad and the South were housed in tenements until placed in a job. By this time the girls would be in debt to the agency for food, shelter and their own personal belongings, which the agent made them deposit with him.[73]

Negro women from the South appeared especially vulnerable to the enterprising techniques of the big-city employment agent, who, through means described below, found it profitable to gain control over his applicants:

> When the newcomers are safely in the agency lodging-house, the runners or ''friends'' of the agency show them the ''sights of the town,'' usually ending up with concert halls; and after such evenings the Negro woman may have lost her chance for honest work. A few days of sight-seeing, during which time she lodges at the agency, and she finds that she owes not only her fare, but from $17.00 to $20.00, for she learns in New York that this sum is the price for her transportation and agent's commission—almost four times the regular fare, which is $5.00. In some agencies she cannot even open her trunk without permission from the

agent, and she must work two months without pay. To whom can she turn? The agent tells her she may leave her trunk without charge, taking only the little she needs, until she sees if she will like the place. At the end of two months, she calls for her trunk and finds fifty cents a week or month is the charge for storage. She has earned no money during those weeks, because of the terms of her contract with the agent; so she forfeits all her possessions. There is cunning in this arrangement! By keeping the girl's baggage and permitting her to use it at the agency the agent holds her indefinitely in his power. He always knows where she is, he places her when she is out of work, or takes her away from one employer for another; he even compels her to give names and addresses of her southern friends, so that he may write to them to come North, using her name as an inducement.[74]

There were some reports that, in a few instances, newly arrived or imported women were sent by some agents to "disreputable houses." This occurred sometimes through carelessness on the part of the agent who failed to look into the job order and sometimes with deliberate collaboration with the house.

White-Collar Agencies

At the turn of this century, there were (and remain today) many different types of specialized private employment agencies. These include agencies established to serve primarily the following occupational groups: teachers (secondary and elementary), nurses, theatrical (actors, stagehands, etc.), barbers and engineers. While each type deserves a full explication, we limit ourselves to a consideration of only one type of agency at this point—the white-collar agency. After we examine the rise of this type of agency and compare it with the other two major types of private employment agencies (manual labor and female domestic), the white-collar agency will be our central focus.

White-collar private employment agencies arose as a specialized entrepreneurial response to a changing work force. The process of industrialization produced a dramatic shift in the percent distribution of occupational groups. In 1900, for instance, farm workers comprised 37.5 percent of the work force, whereas in 1972 they constituted a mere 4.3 percent of the work force. This shift highly favored white-collar workers, as there developed a great need for white-collar workers of all types. White-collar workers in 1900 amounted to only 17.6 percent of the work force. By 1972 they rapidly approached a majority of the work force with 46.6 percent.

Toward the end of the 1800s, white-collar workers seldom obtained their jobs through a private employment agency. The jobs were usually obtained

TABLE 3
Percent Distribution by Major Occupation Group for the Economically Active Civilian Population, 1900-1972

MAJOR OCCUPATION GROUP	1900*	1910*	1920*	1930*	1940*	1950*	1960*	1972†
White-Collar Workers	**17.6**	**21.3**	**24.9**	**29.4**	**31.1**	**36.6**	**42.0**	**46.6**
Professional, technical and kindred	4.3	4.7	5.4	6.8	7.5	8.6	10.8	13.2
Managers, officials and proprietors exc. farm	5.8	6.6	6.6	7.4	7.3	8.7	10.2	9.8
Clerical and kindred	3.0	5.3	8.0	8.9	9.6	12.3	14.5	17.1
sales workers	4.5	4.7	4.9	6.3	6.7	7.0	6.5	6.5
Manual Workers	**35.8**	**38.2**	**40.2**	**39.6**	**39.8**	**41.1**	**37.5**	**35.9**
Craftsmen, foremen and kindred	10.5	11.6	13.0	12.8	12.0	14.1	12.9	13.4
Operatives and kindred workers	12.8	14.6	15.6	15.8	18.4	20.4	18.6	16.6
Laborers, exc. farm and mine	12.5	12.0	11.6	11.0	9.4	6.6	6.0	5.9
Service Workers	**9.0**	**9.6**	**7.8**	**9.8**	**11.7**	**10.5**	**12.6**	**13.2**
Private household workers	5.4	5.0	3.3	4.1	4.7	2.6	3.3	1.1
Service, exc. private household	3.6	4.6	4.5	5.7	7.1	7.9	9.3	11.7
Farm Workers	**37.5**	**30.9**	**27.0**	**21.2**	**17.4**	**11.8**	**7.9**	**4.3**
Farmers and farm managers	19.9	16.5	15.3	12.4	10.4	7.4	4.0	2.1
Farm laborers and foremen	17.7	14.4	11.7	8.8	7.0	4.4	3.9	2.1
Total %	100.0	100.0	100.0	100.0	100.0	100.0	100.0	100.0

*Figures are from: Industrial Union Department, AFL-CIO, Research Department, *Selected Tables Depicting the Changing Character of U.S. Labor Force* (mimeographed, June, 1961), Table 2.
†*Employment and Earnings*, Vol. 19 No. 3, U.S. Department of Labor, Bureau of Labor Statistics (September, 1972), p. 34.

through personal communication with the employer. Sometimes an employer would make it known to his friends that he was looking for a man who could do office work, emit a clean-cut, hard-working appearance and be serious about "company matters." Informal networks, friend to friend, were the circuitry through which such news was transported. Employment middlemen in this area were rare. Since the area of need was small at that time, personal communication through the informal networks was sufficient. In addition, employment agents were of dubious character. The personal recommendation was the chief source of information. The role played by newspapers, of course, promised possible solutions to the information problem of worker and employer finding each other.

As the number of white-collar workers grew, informal networks were determined to break down. Enterprising agents eager to "cash in" on the new labor market began to watch the white-collar market evolve. At first, private employment agents steered clear of the white-collar market largely because the number of available white-collar jobs was dwarfed by the number of white-collar job-seekers. In 1910 a report from the National Employment Exchange, a philanthropic group, commented upon the difference between placing white-collar workers and manual laborers:

> During 1910, the demand for men to do manual work greatly exceeded the supply. Work for more than 4,000 was found in the city, in New York, and in other states. Many more could have been placed had the men been available. It cost $1.93 to get each man his job, over and above the small fee collected. Business depression this year has altered conditons, and not so many positions are open, but it has been established as generally true that the man who is willing to do manual work, skilled or unskilled, can find work if he wants it. There is plenty of room for *him*.
>
> But not so in the mercantile bureau, for office help, salesmen, and similar occupations. The number seeking work of this kind is many times larger than the number of possible places. Positions were found for only 537 out of 4,540 applicants, and the cost of placing each one was $16.40 more than the fee. Many of these successful applicants were forced to accept employment at $5 or $6 a week. New York is flooded with a horde of young men and women who want to do only "genteel" work, and this drugging of the market has forced salaries which the average applicant must accept far below a fair living standard.
>
> Much of this over-supply of mercantile help is due to the young American's desire for easy work and a white collar.[75]

Nevertheless, when it became problematic for employers to locate qualified white-collar workers, employment middlemen became more welcome by employers. One of the first white-collar agents describes in a 1917 article how he entered the business. He was a popular ex-college athlete, who started his work career as a real-estate salesman. His "natural" entry into becoming an employment middleman, specializing in white-collar employees, is discussed in his own words:

In my youth I was the "outside man" for the largest real estate firm in our city. I had been an all-around athlete as a boy and had dabbled in politics before most fellows began to think along that line. Through these circumstances and a natural sociability, I had got a reputation as a "good mixer," and my firm found me valuable because I seemed to know everybody in the city. I was the "scout." I located "prospects" and introduced them to our expert salesmen.

I really liked to meet people and be with them, but after a time this became a sort of burden. So many persons whom one meets in this way want to impose on one! I learned soon that in self-protection I should have to refuse to lend money; but it took me years to learn when to help a man get a job and when to decline to do so.

This getting-a-job favor became the blight of my young life. I knew business men who needed workers, and politicians with jobs to bestow, and whenever a man asked me to help him find a place I usually did so. My reputation as a job-getter spread rapidly; those whom I helped came back and brought their friends. And much of my time was taken up.

One morning the office manager of a big retail dry goods house remarked that he needed a certain type of man for an important position.

"I ought to be able to get one for you," I remarked sarcastically. "I have about a dozen fellows a day haunting me for jobs." "Get me the right man and I'll buy you the best suit of clothes in town," he said.

After we parted I commenced thinking of what he had said. An idea was coming—I was beginning to wonder if there was not some way for me to use my large acquaintanceship to some profit. I sat down and took out a notebook in which I jotted down names and addresses of persons who had asked me to find them jobs. There were two men on the list who seemed qualified for the position. I telephoned them to drop in at the office. The first one, I soon discovered, was not fitted for the place; but after half an hour's conversation with the second I was satisfied he was the right man.

I took him to the office of my friend and said:

"I've got the man. I want you to take him on two weeks' trial, with the understanding that if he is not the one you want you can send him back to me."

Two weeks later I received a check and a note saying, ''Buy yourself that suit. We think J.L. is a jewel.'' A week later the man himself came to me, begging me to accept some token of his gratitude. That man is now a big man in the office force. I had made two friends and a suit of clothes.[76]

The experience was enough for the above writer to decide to leave the real-estate business and work full time as an employment middleman. However, he admitted, ''The idea of becoming an employment agent was distasteful to me.''[77]

The above enterprising white-collar agent also initiated certain practices that were creative and somewhat startling at the time but which are today common practices. First, he insisted that employers pay the fee for his services (similar to the already established practice in domestic servant agencies) because the employer benefits the most out of a good employee.

Second, he embarked on the practice of counseling college students who did not have a clear idea of what career to follow. This group often entered into the business of the family. It was helpful for our white-collar agent to have a trusted and respected relationship with many businessmen in order to facilitate the development of his career as an employment agent. This relationship with employers was useful in recruiting college students as applicants, especially those whose fathers or relatives were already on good terms with the agent.

This example of how one person became a white-collar employment agent is more than a Horatio Alger success story. It reflects social and economic change. Employers were willing to pay the fee for white-collar workers, whereas a few years earlier an agency could find few openings for ''genteel'' work. It appears that the widely distrusted image of employment agencies was taken into account by employers. Relatives or personal recommendations from friends was the main source of recruiting outside of the company (as opposed to inside promotions). But the growing need for office and administrative talent seriously weakened the informal recruitment procedure.

The major difference between the emergence of the white-collar agency and the rudimentary beginnings of manual labor agencies is that in the latter case central meeting places (marketplaces, saloons) evolved into employment agencies, whereas in the former case a central person evolved into an employment agent. The private employment agency office simply became a later version of the human marketplace.

Slowly but surely, white-collar agencies began springing up in every large city. The ''lower echelon'' of white-collar workers were the first main batch of applicants regularly placed through employment agencies. Agencies placing white-collar workers moved to locations and developed counseling and placement procedures that differed dramatically from those of manual labor and domestic servant agencies. Immigrant ghettoes were undesirable locations; few well-qualified white-collar applicants would be attracted to such settings. Agencies featuring male and female secretaries and office clerks were operated within the medium-high-rent office buildings. Not all agencies placing such applicants, however, relinquished the curbside shops. Curbside employment agencies sometimes succeeded in placing office workers.

The history of white-collar agencies is still unfolding. We know from scattered published figures that the growth rate of white-collar agencies was much slower than that of manual labor, female domestic and general agencies until World War II. But after the war white-collar agencies started to multiply rapidly until they overtook all other agencies. Today, 90 percent of the placements made through employment agencies are in the white-collar category.

This chapter was concerned largely with painting a previously unknown historical sketch of the social conditions that made possible the development of job middlemen or private employment agents who perform their duties for commercial profit. Since antiquity there has always been a convenient marketplace where job-seekers and employers could meet one another. Similarly, there is a long history of instances where a job middleman was utilized as an administrative solution to the recruitment and selection of workers, usually when large numbers of workers were needed and some traveling was necessary. Such was the case in ancient Sumer, where temple priests served as job middlemen.

We traced the social forerunners of private employment agents from the temples of ancient Sumer, through medieval Europe where traveling recruiters (locators) induced workers to leave their homeland in hopes of finding better work, to the United States where job middlemen induced many people to come to the land of plenty for ''glorious'' jobs and where other job middlemen processed anxious job-seekers. A description of the turn of the century private employment agencies is gleaned from the writings of early American sociologists, muckrakers and social reformers.

Eager entrepreneurs easily set up private employment agencies where agents provided the better service to either employers or applicants, depending upon who paid the fee and which commodity was more scarce. The most disadvantaged applicants (usually immigrants) were the most vulnerable to the private agents.

Increased mobility among workers and a change in the legal definition of work converged with expanding entrepreneurial consciousness. This made possible the growth of the social role of private employment agents.

NOTES

1. Gustave Glotz, *Ancient Greece at Work* (New York: Barnes and Noble, 1965), p. 278.

2. Matthew 20.

3. Henri Pirenne, *Economic and Social History of Medieval Europe* (New York : Harcourt, Brace, 1937), p. 187.

4. Theodore Thomas Cowgill, "The Employment Agencies," (M.A. thesis, University of Chicago, 1928), p. 20.

5. Although contemporary users of some manual labor employment agencies refer to them as "slave markets," we do not include slave traders as forerunners of private employment agents. Our focus is on job-seekers and their relationship with agents, which is markedly different from the relationship of a slave with his trader. Structurally, however, there is some similiarity; an agent dealing in human beings sells them to an employer, and an employer "buys" laborers from an agent.

6. This is from records found in the ruins of Senkereh (the ancient Larsa). *New York Times*, May 16, 1920, p. 6.

7. James Westfall Thompson, *Feudal Germany* (Chicago: University of Chicago Press, 1928), p. 539.

8. Helmold, *The Chronicle of the Slavs*, trans. Frances J. Tschan (New York: Columbia University Press, 1935).

9. J.H. Clapham and Eileen Power, eds., *The Cambridge Economic History of Europe from the Decline of the Roman Empire*, vol. 1 (Cambridge, England: Oxford University Press, 1941), p. 462.

10. Ibid.

11. Ibid.

12. Thompson, *Feudal Germany*, p. 511.

13. Clapham and Power, *Cambridge Economic History*, p. 462.

14. This is an interesting reversal of the contemporary pattern of retaining a skilled cadre during seasonal slumps and picking up less-skilled workers as activity increases.

15. Abbot E. Smith, *Colonists in Bondage* (Gloucester, Mass.: Peter Smith, 1965), p. 45.

16. Ibid., pp. 45-46.

17. William Petyt, *Britannia Languens* (1680), p. 238, as quoted in E.S. Furniss, *The Position of the Laborer in a System of Nationalism* (New York: Kelley, 1957), pp. 16, 17 (italics ours).

18. See Adam Smith, *An Inquiry into the Nature and Cases of The Wealth of Nations*, ed. James E. Thorold (Clarenden: Oxford, 1880).

19. Karl Polanyi, *The Great Transformation* (New York: Beacon, 1957), pp. 103-5.

20. Ibid., p. 105.

21. Ibid.

22. William Weedon, *Economic and Social History of New England 1620-1789*, vol. 1 (1890; reprint ed., New York: Hillary House, 1963), p. 193.

23. Many people were sentenced to transportation to the colonies for minor criminal offenses, including political and religious offenses. Felons were even allowed to become indentured servants as an alternative to hanging. These servants went through the same general process but are not discussed here because they were unwilling employees, as were slaves.

24. Smith, *Colonists in Bondage*, passim.

25. Ibid., p. 58.

26. Ibid.

27. Ibid.

28. Ibid.

29. Ibid.

30. Ibid., p. 67ff.

31. Ibid., p. 74.

32. Ibid., p. 60.

33. The absence of a valid, available history of private employment agencies is highlighted by the comments made by Anna Reed in a major work on occupational placement procedures: "The Commercial agency as a medium for the distribution of labor in this country has no authentic history. Its initial efforts are even more difficult to uncover than are those of philanthropic agencies, that both responded to a demand for some systematic method of bringing the needs of employers and workers together, and that they began operations during the same period of time—about 1820." Anna Y. Reed, *Occupational Placement* (Ithaca, N.Y.: Cornell University Press, 1946), p. 25.

34. *State Laws Regulating Private Employment Agencies*, Fact Sheet No. 5 (Washington, D.C.: U.S. Department of Labor, Bureau of Labor Statistics, April 1966), p. 1.

35. "So You're Opening An Employment Agency!" (Detroit: National Employment Assoc., n.d.), p. 2.

36. Cowgill, "Employment Agencies," p. 20.

37. *New York Evening Times*, September 18, 1851, p. 3.

38. *Voice of Industry*, January 2, 1846, quoted from the *Cabotville Chronicle*, cf. John R. Commons, et al., *A Documentary History of American Industrial Development*, vol. 9 (Cleveland: A.H. Clark, 1910), p. 141.

39. George S. White, *Memoir of Samuel Slater and A History of the Rise and Progress of the Cotton Manufacture in England and America* (Philadelphia: n.p., 1836).

40. Commons, *Industrial Development*, vol. 10, p. 73ff.

41. *New York Evening Times*, January 2, 1846, p. 3.

42. E.L. Bogart, "Public Employment Offices in the United States and Germany," *Quarterly Journal of Economics*, Spring 1900, pp. 341-77; Frances A. Kellor, *Out of Work* (New York: Putnam, 1915).

43. Edwin Anders, "Employment Agencies in Portland," *The Survey*, July 11, 1914, p. 289.

44. Grace Abbott, "The Chicago Employment Agency and the Immigrant Worker," *The American Journal of Sociology* 14 (November 1908): p. 289.

45. Ibid., p. 292.

46. Ibid., p. 293.

47. Ibid.

48. Ibid., p. 294.

49. Ibid., p. 295.

50. Ibid.

51. Ibid.

52. *New York Times*, May 22, 1939, p. 41.

53. Ibid.

54. Ibid.

55. Kellor, *Out of Work*, p. 157.

56. Ibid., pp. 158-59.

57. Ibid., pp. 160-61.

58. Ibid., p. 161.

59. Abbott, "Employment Agency and Immigrant Worker," p. 296.

60. Ibid.

61. Kellor, *Out of Work*, p. 158.

62. Ibid.

63. Ibid.

64. Ibid., pp. 194-95.

65. *New York Times*, September 27, 1872, p. 11 (italics theirs).

66. Kellor, *Out of Work*, p. 159.

67. Anonymous, "A Vicious Circle," *Atlantic Monthly* 31 (January-June 1923): 566-69.

68. Kellor, *Out of Work*, pp. 200-4.

69. Ibid.

70. Ibid.

71. Ibid.

72. Frances A. Kellor, "Assisted Emigration From the South, The Women,"

Charities 15 (October 7, 1905): 11-14.

73. Ibid.

74. Ibid., p. 14.

75. "The Job of Getting Jobs," *World's Work* 23 (July 1911): 1454-55 (italics theirs).

76. "Getting Jobs for Other People," *The American Magazine* 84 (November 1917): 138-39.

77. Ibid., p. 139.

2

ABUSES BY PRIVATE
EMPLOYMENT AGENCIES

In their pursuit of profits, some private employment agencies have engaged in activities deemed abusive by the "moral crusaders" of the day (e.g., journalists, judges, legislators and a variety of social reformers).[1] The history of private employment agencies in this country and abroad has been characterized by charges of business abuses. This chapter identifies and describes the types of abuses typically attributed to private employment agencies.

Of course, the extent of abuses will never be known, for reasons articulated by Howard S. Becker:

> Those who commit deviant acts protect themselves from prying outsiders. Deviance within organized conventional institutions is often protected by a kind of cover-up. Thus, members of the professions do not ordinarily speak about cases of unethical practices in public.[2]

This "covering-up" process has been typical of private employment agencies, according to William Papier, director of research and statistics, Ohio Bureau of Employment Services. As one of the most visibly concerned researchers on the impact of private employment agencies in the country, Mr. Papier states in a recent report on private employment agencies in Ohio: "Although operations of private employment agencies greatly affect the public interest, an aura of secrecy has long surrounded their activities."[3]

We will examine abuses by all three types of private employment agents (manual labor, female domestic and white collar) during their history. After World War II, the emphasis will be primarily on white-collar agencies

43

because most of the data gathered on contemporary abuses involves white-collar agents and because the white-collar agency is of central concern today.

In 1912, the U.S. Bureau of Labor compiled a list of the various types of abuses committed by private employment agencies:

1. Charging a fee and failing to find work for the applicant.
2. Sending applicant where no work exists.
3. Sending applicant to distant point where unsatisfactory work exists but whence the applicant will not return on account of the expense involved.
4. Collusion between the agent and the employers, whereby the applicant is given a few days work and then discharged to make way for a new workman, the agent and the employer dividing the fee.
5. Charging exhorbitant fees or giving jobs to such applicants as contribute extra fees, presents, etc.
6. Inducing workers, particularly girls who have been placed, to leave, pay another fee and get a "better job."

Misrepresentation

The most frequent abuse appears to be misrepresentation of the terms and conditions of employment,[5] which usually emerges initially in the form of misleading advertisements. It has been written and taken for granted that advertising often distorts the truth, attempting to mislead the audience. A further indictment upon misleading advertisement is unnecessary here, but an analysis of advertising techniques of private employment agents would help us understand how employment agents are able to misrepresent the terms and conditions of employment.

As we examine the history of private employment agencies, we find an early reliance upon misleading advertisements. Such ads proved successful in recruiting large numbers of applicants who often had left their homes in search of jobs in the United States because they were encouraged by an ad placed by a private employment agent in an American newspaper sold in foreign countries. Often the job in the ad was a nonexistent situation. Some immigrants were led to believe, by both ads and foreign agents, that "the streets were lined with gold" and consequently "went from job to job in search of this place."[6]

Kellor notes the tendency for employment agents at the turn of the twentieth century to advertise with "little regard for the truth."[7] Some typical advertisements of that time are:

Wanted—500 laborers for Railroad work in Missouri and Indiana; free fares. Marble cutters and carvers; no union. Porter who can speak German. We have positions for all classes of help.

Wanted—500 Railroad laborers, company and contract work; free fare; low rates to New Orleans and points South. Farm hands $25 to $30 per. mo. and board. Good home for winter, also other jobs near city.[8]

Abbott presents several concrete cases involving gross misrepresentation by Chicago employment agents around 1908. One such story reveals the drama of ruthless deception of vulnerable men and women:

During the past year a railroad has been building from Searcy in north-central Arkansas to Leslie, about ninety miles farther west. Great numbers of men were sent from Chicago to Leslie to work on this road. We found two groups who had been there. One of these was made up of Hungarians. There were fifty-three men and two women—one of these had a baby—who expected to act as cooks for the gang. They were shipped April 14, by a Chicago agent, through a St. Louis agent. They paid the Chicago agent fourteen dollars apiece and were promised steady work at $1.40 a day. When they reached Leslie this is what happened, according to the story told by the men. They were told that the work was twenty-five miles from there. They walked to this place but the foreman only laughed at them and said he had no work for any such number. He finally put to work fifteen men and the woman who was unencumbered with the baby. The rest were told there would be work for them later on but they were without money or food and so could not stay. They started to walk back to Chicago where more such jobs are always to be had! At the end of the third day the woman gave out and the men pooled their money and sent her home on the railroad. Then they scattered so as to find work on the way. Two of them were shot by the police in St. Louis and when last heard from were in a hospital there. The rest of them eventually reached Chicago.[9]

In Cowgill's investigation of employment agencies in 1928 a similar tendency is noted. He simply states, "There is some foul play through the use of the want ad."[10] He then goes on to substantiate his remark:

Some agencies advertise for applicants in such a way that the ad cannot be told from an ordinary help wanted advertisement. When the applicant enters the agency he is requested to sign a regular application blank, and it is only if he states that he is answering an ad for a job that he is interviewed as a possible employee of the agency. Sometimes jobs are advertised at an inflated figure, and the fact circumvented by adding the

phrase, "To the right party" in the ad. Often these ads are designed to
make it appear that the agency has more actual jobs waiting than they
really have. Some jobs that require considerable expenses on the part of
the employee, but having a salary considerably above the average for that
type of position can be advertised for several days at the apparently
attractive figure, and doubtless attract many applicants.[11]

How did the agent deal with the applicant who was misled by an ad,
especially if the applicant had to travel a great distance? In some cases, the
agent would simply say that particular job was no longer available. Then the
agent might make an attempt to interest the applicant in what was available.
In other cases, the agent would already have the applicant in his debt,
because the agent might pay the traveling expenses or have a signed contract.
We noted in the last chapter that in the case of the female domestic agencies,
immigrant women would sometimes have their luggage impounded by the
agent until a job was accepted. Many manual labor agents would send the
applicants too far for them to return easily. Thus, the agents probably did not
have to develop the skills of redefining the situation to applicants whom they
misled because the applicants did not often return and complain.

Undoubtedly there are numerous instances when the agent neglects to
acquaint himself with the specific working conditions of the job he represents to the applicant. In this situation, it may not be conscious misrepresentation. In other cases, it is a matter of deliberate falsifying. In a survey
conducted by the New York Industrial Survey Commission in 1930, the
activities of private employment agencies "witness after witness," testifying under oath, described "flagrant abuses" practiced by some agents.[12] For
example, one witness describes a fictitious job offer:

The Witness: He sent me to five or six jobs and they needed nobody.
Furthermore they had not sent down for anybody, but he had my money
and he said: "Don't worry, keep cool, and I will give you a job."
Chairman Turman: He did not give you a job?
The Witness: He did not. I was going there for over a week and I got tired
of going there, and I wasted several hours sitting up in his office, and yet
he had down on the slate downstairs the very jobs that I was looking for.[13]

Today, nearly 40 states have passed laws prohibiting agencies from
placing false ads. But such laws are difficult to enforce. Private employment
agents find that advertising nonexistent jobs serves a valuable business
function. One valuable function, according to Margolin, is that such ads help
agents "force their way" into new fields.:

Take the employment agent who wants to foist his services upon some part of the publishing industry, although he is new to that business. First, he advertises positions for writers, editors, copy editors, researchers, proofreaders, and production people. Since these positions exist only in his imagination, he can promise whopping salaries, fringe benefits, and guaranteed opportunities for advancement. Sometimes he places the ad with only a box number for the applicant to send his resume to. The agent answers none of the letters he gets, as anyone who has answered these blind ads is well aware.

Once the agent has a thick inventory of names, he combs trade journals devoted to the publishing industry for Help Wanted ads placed directly by the hiring company. He then calls the employer and shows him the piles of resumes of ''people he represents.'' Of course, all these job hunters will fork over the placement fee. So the employer can meet these qualified, ambitious people without any obligation. Few companies resist this sales pitch.[14]

Thus, one purpose of false advertising for the private employment agency is to generate new business in the human marketplace.

The private employment agency I studied as a participant observer frequently engaged in misleading advertisements. The ads were mainly intended to bring in new applicants. Once inside the agency, the applicant was directed away from the glamorous job described in the ad and into a more accessible one. In one instance, a 35-year-old man had come into the agency seeking a job advertised falsely. The agency's newspaper ad described a public relations position with an international transportation company. In order to qualify, the ad stated, a person should be a college graduate and be able to get along well with others. The 35-year-old applicant had been up to this time a television repairman and received his degree in night college, but he came in convinced that he could do the work described in the misleading ad. In reality, the job did not exist; it was made up to bring in new applicants. However, the agency could not inform the eager applicant of this fact. Instead, I was told to try to have him look into a job that was more directly related to his experience, much to his disappointment.

Fee-Splitting

Stated simply, an employment agent and an employer agree to divide the fee of an applicant, who is kept on the payroll for a limited time. In order to maximize profits, a turnover of employees is accelerated through firing. Agents are reputed to have made frequent arrangements with railroad con-

tractors in the early 1900s.[15] In the recent past, foremen often received part
of the fee for hiring workers through an agent when the worker paid the fee.
The New York Commission uncovered much evidence of this practice. In
one case, the foreman each week discharged one-third of the workers for
seemingly no reason.[16] An expert on employment work offered the following related testimony:

> I spent two weeks on one case and got quite a few affidavits. There was a
> working agreement between the foreman and a fee-charging agency,
> where they were splitting fees. There were 500 men working in this plant
> in a period of six weeks, and they were charged a fee of $5. At that time
> there were complaints by men that they paid a fee of $5, and they were
> allowed to work a week, and then they were laid off, and a new bunch put
> in, and the fee was split between the agency and the employer of that firm.
> That was proven by affidavits of the men who saw the actual payment of
> money by the fee-charging agent to the employer of that firm.[17]

The extent of fee-splitting today is probably less than it was in the early
1900s, largely because of the disappearance of large labor contractors and
the increased risks of detection by a governmental agency or moral crusader.

Proselyting

Private employment agents typically engage in a practice known in the
field as proselyting, or "head hunting." This refers to attempts by agents to
influence former applicants and potential recruits to leave their present jobs
in order to accept another through the agency. In such a case, the agent
normally has a specific job opening in mind when he contacts a former or
potential applicant. Supreme Court Justice Brandeis, in a dissenting opinion
concerning the legality of the state of Washington to outlaw private employment agencies (see chapter 3) in 1917 notes that proselyting is a
universal custom among agents:

> Investigations show, however, that instead of relieving unemployment
> and reducing irregularity, these employment agencies actually serve to
> congest the labor market and to increase idleness and irregularity of
> employment. They are interested primarily in the fees they can earn, and
> if they can earn more by bringing workers to an already overcrowded city,
> they do so. Again, it is an almost universal custom among private
> employment agents to fill vacancies by putting in them people who are
> working at other places. In this way new vacancies are created and more
> fees can be earned.[18]

Today, employers encourage proselyting by agents, especially when a person with special skills is needed. Catering to the special needs of employers is an important function for the professional searchers, head hunters or "executive recruiters" who specialize in proselyting. Since it would be awkward (and illegal in some respects) for an employer to directly contact a person working for another firm when the purpose is to learn about the worker's view of his present job, some employers in this situation ask an agent with whom they have done satisfactory business in the past to "take a reading" on the specific worker.

A very successful woman agent with over ten years experience, who identified herself as a "professional searcher," told me how this kind of proselyting is done:

R: Now, I can be accused of this (proselyting). But, you take a company that has, we'll say, because we're talking about ethnic groups now, they have a man that the company only has in there for window-dressing; and maybe he has all the capabilities in the world, and he is drawing a good salary—being very well-paid for nothing, because they are not using his capabilities. Well, the man obviously isn't stupid, and he knows something is wrong, but he doesn't quite know what it is. So, a company, or an individual, will approach someone like myself, and they'll want a "reading" on this individual.

I: What do you mean "a reading"?

R: Well, to know what his feeling is, if he realizes he is being taken advantage of, and that he is not having the opportunity to advance his capabilities at all. He's not even able to keep himself in the state of the art. And so, and as I said, a company cannot take and approach this. If they do, they are crazy, but they will seek someone out like myself. Not that they are trying to get him away, they are just trying to make him aware that there are opportunities open to him that will give him the advancement, and give him the opportunity to maintain the state of the art. And, then, this is the way it is done.

Proselyting is becoming an increasing practice among private employment agents, primarily because more big business organizations are willing to pay large fees to the agent who can locate a top executive. Despite this growth there are still protesting voices raised against the practice. William Papier, for example, in 1972 wrote in a research paper circulated among researchers interested in private employment agencies:

The immediate past President of the Ohio Private Employment Service Association, testifying at a public hearing conducted by the Ohio Advisory Council on Employment Security on June 1, 1972, indicated that private agencies concentrate primarily on persons already employed, but interested in better jobs. Snelling and Snelling, one of the larger franchise operators of private agencies—which claims to be the "World's Largest Professional Employment Service"—has repeatedly reported in classified newspaper ads that "Eighty percent of the people we place are already employed."

Where both employers and employees are satisfied, however, turnover is undesirable. No employee, however, should be denied the initiative in seeking a better job, nor should any employer be prohibited in taking the initiative to find better employees. Yet it is not in the public interest for private agencies to phone or otherwise contact specific employed workers who have no recent record of desire to change, in an effort to stimulate interest in new jobs elsewhere. Such practices should be forbidden by statute.[19]

Discrimination

The abuse of most recent public concern is that of racial, religious and sex discrimination. It was demonstrated in the preceding chapter that private agents have tended to treat the most vulnerable applicants the worst. The most vulnerable, of course, are those groups discriminated and disadvantaged in society at large. Until recently, all types of employment agents have accepted racially, religiously and sex-biased job orders without significant public protest. With the advent of the civil rights movement and ensuing legislation, however, the government has been able to pressure agencies to deal with applicants and job orders without overt discrimination. Indeed, when employers themselves have felt the need to change their hiring practices, the change has sometimes been from overt to covert discrimination, with the aid of the private agent. As long as client-employers discriminate, private employment agents will do likewise. Profit-seeking agents seldom feel a personal obligation to exert an extra effort to place a person who is a member of a group that is discriminated against in society. This has led to the development of certain business practices by agents to identify the "difficult to place" applicants.

For example, an assistant attorney-general in charge of the New York State Civil Rights Bureau, Mrs. Shirley Siegel, subpoenaed the records of one of the largest private agencies in New York in 1963. She discovered that Negro applicants were identified by the code NFU, which meant Not For Us. Job orders often bore the note, "No NFUs."[20] A similar code was used by another agency: POK (Persons of Color). As the woman attorney-general began prosecuting, it was found that the agencies changed their practices from obvious codes to less obvious signs (e.g., underlining the name of

TABLE 4
1968 Survey of Private Agenices
Accepting Discriminatory Job Orders*

City	No. of Agencies Surveyed	No. Accepting Order	% Accepting Order
Atlanta	42	41	97
Chicago	106	101	95
Kansas City	55	49	89
Los Angeles	77	66	86
Miami	38	38	100
New York	91	60	67
Omaha	14	14	100
Phoenix	34	32	94
Total	457	401	88

Source: *Rights*, The Anti-Defamation League, February, 1968, p. 24.

certain applicants). As one agent admitted to Wayne Morse's investigating committee of private employment agencies in 1962, ''It is not unusual for us to have employers request white and Negro workers for the same job at different salaries, paying the white worker $10 to $15 more a week.''[21] Thus, the agent does not find it unusual to cater to the wishes of the employer.

Governmental attempts toward controlling discrimination in hiring has influenced many employers to turn to private employment agents in order to continue past policies. It is illegal for an employer to advertise, ''only whites need apply,'' but he could call many private agencies and ask for ''a white Protestant,'' ''an all-American girl'' or ''a man to meet the public.'' Knowledge of such practices spurred the Anti-Defamation League to conduct a series of surveys to determine the approximate percentage of private agencies that would accept clearly discriminatory job orders. Their most systematic survey began in 1968.[22] A job order calling for ''a white gentile secretary'' was given over the telephone to 457 private employment agencies in eight major American cities. The agencies in the sample were those who advertised in the Sunday newspapers for secretaries. The results of the survey are presented in Table 4.

The total percentage of agencies accepting the order (88 percent) is somewhat distorted by the relatively low percentage in New York (67 percent), with 91 agencies surveyed. The median percentage accepting (94 percent) is not affected by the extreme scores.

Such survey information is useful, because it demonstrates the willingness of the agencies to serve the employer, even when the employer is a stranger calling over the phone. Some of the comments from the agents are noteworthy:

> *Chicago:*
> "We don't place colored."
> "That's exactly what I was going to ask you."
> "White Gentiles are always most capable."
> *Los Angeles:*
> "Legally, no. Diplomatically, yes."
> "Will not show on order, secret between you and me."
> "Hope so, though really not allowed."
> "I'll send the 'All-American girl'."
> *New York:*
> "There would be no problem."
> "Not allowed to take such an order, but will try to help out."
> "I know how to mark this."
> "This is understandable. Can be gotten around."[23]

About one-half of the agents who rejected the order cited the law as the main reason. In a similar survey by the league, a San Francisco agent replied: "No, I couldn't discriminate. Firms are not supposed to have prejudices against anyone. It is against the law. Don't you know that?"[24] The ADL also surveyed, for comparative purposes, state employment agencies in the above cities. None accepted the job order.

It should be noted that this data was gathered by strangers to the agencies. It would be logical to assume that discriminatory job orders from regular client-employers would be greeted by a higher rate of acceptance. If employers desire a racially represented work force, the agents would help them find the necessary workers, assuming it would be economically profitable for the agents. Indeed, a somewhat analoguous situation has occurred in many industries which depend upon governmental contract work because of the civil rights legislation of the 1960s.

There is some evidence to suggest that agencies engaging in discriminatory practices are also very likely to engage in the other types of abuses. Discrimination, as a form of exploitation, may be symbolically important in an agency's decision to practice different forms of abuses. For example, in the spring of 1969 the attorney-general of California sought an injunction against private employment agencies in the Los Angeles area for alleged discriminatory practices plus civil monetary penalties for their allegedly false and misleading representation.[25] According to the complaint:

employment agencies had regularly refused to receive applications from Negro applicants and applicants with Spanish surnames. The Attorney

General charged the agency used a special code to designate application forms it accepted from some Negro and Spanish surname applicants. In addition, the agency was charged with cooperating in discriminatory practices by employers. The suit alleged that the agency discussed the racial background of applicants with prospective employers and confined the selection of applicants to those who were racially acceptable.[26]

The Extent of Agency Abuse

Scandals concerning the above abuses have occasionally emerged in newspaper articles during the past 100 years. The articles implied that the vast majority of agencies were guilty. Little space has been devoted to pointing out the commendable, ethical practices of other agents. Let us provide some natural, honest balance to the historical story. Even in the field of manual labor there were responsible, honest agents. The most famous of these was run by Mrs. S.J. Atwood, called "laborers' big sister."[27] She became an agent in the 1890s at the suggestion of a division superintendant of Union Pacific Railroad when she became a widow with a child and an aged father. At the time agent abuses were rampant, especially those affiliated with railroads.

She opened her first office in Denver, and her success enabled her to open offices rapidly in nine states. By 1916, her agencies had placed men in every state. She also operated commissaries from Montana to Virginia, where men lived in tents and boxcars. She was on a first-name basis with the men and served as a letter-writer for the illiterate. Her methods were commended by *The Survey*, a social welfare magazine that had been urging the abolishment of employment agencies for 20 years.[28] One instance cited by the magazine involved an order for 25 workers that Mrs. Atwood received from Albany. By chance, she discovered that five other agencies had the same order. If each agency sent 25 workers, then 150 would be the total. She called the company to find out if there were 150 or 25 openings. Because she had been told there were only 25, she refused to send applicants.

While muckrakers and others periodically criticized employment agents, many agents complained. The agents upheld the "bad apple theory"—a few spoil the image of all. Agents also protest that journalists and social reformers fail to distinguish between types of employment agencies. White-collar agents typically complain that the negative public image of the general agency should not be permitted to darken their more ethical, professional practices. One highly reputable woman agent in California expressed her concern over the normal business practices of the general agency, "I am ashamed to say this; in fact, it has always kind of embarrassed me."

Clearly, there have been and are abuses by private agents. Yet, no one knows how many agencies are, or were, guilty of malpractices. Only one empirical study examining this problem has been found, but it is confined to California for the year 1937.[29] Nevertheless, the data based upon registered complaints is noteworthy. For the year 1937, 410 complaints were recorded by the Labor Commission, 11 made by agencies against applicants and employers. Almost three-fourths of the manual agencies were involved. About 90 percent of the complaints were against the general agencies. In 80 percent of the cases, the commissioner ordered either a whole or partial fee refund. Refusal to refund fee constituted 90 percent of the complaints. The reasons for demanding a refund were: (1) misrepresentation of the kind of work, rate of wages or living accommodations; (2) failure to inform applicant that a labor strike was in progress; (3) applicant discharged during period in which agency is required to refund fee; and (4) no job where applicant was sent.

Looking at the data another way, there is some indirect support to the notion of an existing group of responsible agencies in the year 1937, since 60 percent of the commercial and 25 percent of the manual labor agencies had no complaints filed against them. In fact, two-thirds of the manual agencies had less than five complaints. Nevertheless, the data suggests there were more than a few "bad apples" spoiling the rest.

The California study was conducted during the Depression. The relationship between types and extent of abuses is uncertain, but some scholars who addressed themselves to the subject believe that depression breeds greater worker exploitation by job middlemen.[30] With the growth of white-collar and professional agencies in times of affluence, other forms of abuses, such as proselyting, may take prominence.

There will always be difficulty in determining to what extent human beings have been fooled. Often the consciousness of being fooled makes one feel foolish. Foolish-feeling people seldom desire to make public their gullibility, which would serve to confirm their feeling further. Therefore, many "victims" of private employment agents choose to remain hidden from official registry, even when they may have lost something (money, time or both) in their relationship with the agent. A historical example is taken from Abbott.[31] She tells of "a bright young fellow of twenty-two," who froze his foot on his way back to Chicago from Wyoming where an agent sent him to report for work, but where none existed. His leg had to be amputated. He was, then, crippled for life. Yet, "he feels not so much resentment against the agent who sent him as shame that he should have been so ignorant of the climate of Wyoming and humiliation that he should be such an easy victim."[32] The ways of people may not have changed greatly since the bright young man lost his leg 50 years ago. To the extent that such shame overrides the desire to complain to the government, abuses by employment agents will continue to go unrecorded in many cases. As long as employers reward agents for practicing discrimination and related abuses, some profit-seeking agents will oblige them.

NOTES

1. For an explanation of "moral crusaders" see Howard S. Becker, *Outsiders* (New York: The Free Press, 1963).

2. Ibid., pp. 168-69

3. William Papier, "Private Employment Agencies in Ohio," Ohio Bureau of Employment Services, 1973, p. 11.

4. Cowgill, "Employment Agencies," pp. 133-34

5. Justice Brandeis dissenting in Adams v. Tanner, 244 U.S. (1916).

6. Frances A. Kellor, "Immigration and Household Labor: A Study of Sinister Social Conditions," *Charities* 12 (February 6, 1904); 151-52.

7. Ibid., p. 52.

8. Kellor, *Out of Work*, p. 167.

9. Abbott, "Employment Agency and Immigrant Worker," pp. 297-98.

10. Cowgill, "Employment Agencies," p. 134.

11. Ibid., pp. 134-35.

12. George H. Trafton, "Employment Agencies Officially Exposed," *American Labor Legislation Review* 20 (March 1930): 27-34.

13. Ibid., p. 28.

14. Malcolm Margolin, "Help Wanted: Honest, Intelligent People to Run Employment Agencies," *Fact*, November-December 1966, p. 44.

15. Abbott, "Employment Agency and Immigrant Worker," p. 297.

16. Trafton, "Agencies Exposed," p. 29.

17. Ibid., p. 30.

18. Adams v. Tanner.

19. Papier, "Agencies in Ohio," p. 9

20. Margolin, "Help Wanted," p. 40.

21. Ibid.

22. The Anti-Defamation League, *Rights*, February 1968, pp. 23-24.

23. Ibid., p. 24.

24. Ibid.

25. CCH, *Employment Practices Guide*, Report #15, April 25, 1969, p. 4.

26. Ibid.

27. "Employment Agencies, Socialism and Unionism on the Stand," *The Survey*, May 30, 1914; "Mrs. Atwood Has Put More Than a Million Men to Work," *American Magazine* 101 (June 1926): 24-25; and "Mrs. Atwood—Laborers' Big Sister," *Illustrated World* 24 (February 1916):806-9.

28. "Employment Agencies, Socialism and Unionism on the Stand," see footnote 27.

29. Emily H. Huntington, *Doors To Jobs* (Los Angeles: University of California Press, 1942).

30. Shelby M. Harrison, *Public Employment Offices* (New York: Russell Sage Foundation, 1924).

31. Abbott, "Employment Agency and Immigrant Worker," pp. 298-99.

32. Ibid., p. 299.

3

SOCIAL CONTROL OF PRIVATE EMPLOYMENT AGENCIES

Movement Toward Regulation

During the early stages of the development of private employment agencies in the United States, few attempts were made by either municipal or state governments to directly control their activities.[1] However, as the abuses became more widespread and visible[2] state and local governments began to respond to the mounting pressure of various social and political groups that were concerned with the plight of the workingman at the hands of private employment agents. Increasingly, the state legislatures, cognizant of the social problems arising from the exploitation of job-seekers by profit-seeking private employment agents, began to enact a wide array of ordinances and regulations aimed at bringing the employment agency industry under the supervision and control of the government.

By 1914, 24 states attempted *direct* regulation of the activities of private employment agencies and 19 states used *indirect* regulation[3] in the form of establishing state or municipal *free public employment agencies* designed to compete with the private agencies, which will be discussed later in this chapter. By 1928, all but nine states had provided in some manner for the regulation of private agencies.[4]

A parallel movement occurred in other nations that had also been confronted with the problems arising from the unhampered activities of private employment agencies. In 1913 the Canadian Labor Congress called for the complete suppression of private employment agencies.[5] The first official International Labor Conference of the League of Nations made a similar resolution a few years later. Germany had become so concerned with the disruptive influence of private employment agencies upon the labor market that in 1922 the German government arranged for the abolition of all private employment agencies in Germany within ten years. Austria met the problems created by private employment agencies by refusing to issue any new licenses after World War I. By 1926 Finland, Romania and Bulgaria had provided for the complete abolition of private employment agencies.[6] Between 1910 and 1930 there seemed to emerge a general consensus among the nations dealing with the private employment agency industry that this industry should be strictly controlled, if not entirely prohibited.

In addition to concern with specific abuses perpetrated by these agents upon job-seekers, there was a general feeling that the unregulated private employment agency industry contributed to, and at times encouraged, unemployment within the labor market. In 1914, the U.S. Commission on Industrial Relations report to the U.S. Congress discussed these problems:

> instead of relieving unemployment and reducing irregularity, these employment agencies actually serve to conquest the labor market and to increase idleness and irregularity of employment. They are interested primarily in the fees they can earn, and if they can earn more by bringing workers to an already overcrowded city, they do so. Again, it is an almost universal custom among private employment agents to fill vacancies by putting in them people who are working at other places. In this way new vacancies are created and more fees can be earned.[7]

The commission also commented on fee-charging:

> The fees which private employment offices must charge are carriers which prevent the proper flow of labor into channels where it is needed and are a direct influence in keeping men idle. In the summer when employment is plentiful, the fees are as low as 25 cents, and men are even referred to work free of charge. But this must necessarily be made up in the winter, when work is scarce. At such times, when men need work most badly, the private employment offices put up their fees and keep the unemployed from going to work until they can pay . . . .[8]

A similar reaction came from Labor Department agent in Washington:

> The complaint against the private office is almost universal. The experience of this office is that private agencies charge all that the traffic will

bear and that in hard times, when work is scarce and the worker poverty-stricken, the fee is placed so high as to be almost prohibitive, and the agencies take longer chances, sometimes sending men on only a rumor, depending on their financial straits to make it impossible to return.[9]

These techniques of the private agencies were regarded not only as exploitation of the particular workingman-client but also as devices that served to inhibit the free flow of labor in times of serious unemployment. Consequently, practices of private employment agencies were deemed a source undermining the stability of the labor market.

There developed a strong degree of sentiment against this industry, which profited from the dire needs of those persons seeking work. There was much feeling that ''this necessity of paying for the privilege of going to work, and paying more the more urgently the job is needed, not only keeps people unnecessarily unemployed, but seems foreign to the spirit of American freedom and opportunity.''[10]

The need for regulation was enhanced not only by the profound effect of these agencies upon the labor market and the economy in general but also by the very nature of the business, which provided a very fertile ground for unscrupulous business practices. One labor expert noted this fertility:

> commercial agencies are under certain peculiar temptations. Employment agencies may be opened by an outlay of but little capital and current expenditures are very small. Relationship with the laborers is not continuous and an unscrupulous manager is therefore not to the same degree as in most businesses under the necessity of maintaining the good will of his constantly changing customers.[11]

The combination of a highly vulnerable clientele and the low degree of skill of expertise necessary to open and maintain a private employment agency created the image of an industry riddled with abusive and unscrupulous practices. Despite this negative image and the wealth of facts that supported it, obtaining governmental regulation was frought with political and legal complications, largely because of the precedent-setting nature of such regulation. Indeed, a close examination of the history of governmental regulation of private employment agencies provides a case study for understanding the interaction between the legislature and the judiciary over governmental control of private enterprise. A detailed history of governmental regulation in this area can be gleaned from specific case and statutory law, following Jerome Hall's advice on how to write legal history: ''For each ultimate link in the chain of its (law) history is a specific case or statute.''[12] In order to make sociological sense out of such case and statutory law, we

must first endeavor to understand the sociolegal climate in which developed
the idea that private employment agencies should be regulated by government.

The Sociolegal Climate of the Late Nineteenth Century

Toward the last quarter of the last century, legislative attempts to enact
laws designed to meet the growing social problems arising from changing
conditions due to urbanization and industrialization came into conflict with
prevailing legal and social philosophies. Early attempts to regulate the
practices of private employment agencies were routed off by the Supreme
Court with declarations of "unconstitutionality" because of the traditional
interpretation of law and justice that stemmed from the influence of historical ties with England.

As in the English judicial system, the notion of common law weighed
heavily upon American legal minds. In the Anglo-American legal tradition,
the common law is regarded as the embodiment of eternal, universal ideals
of justice which in earlier times have been termed "natural laws." In the
United States, we operate within a legal system dominated by a Constitution,
or supreme law of the land. Fundamental to each of these concepts of
law—natural, common or constitutional law—is the attitude that the law is
not created by man but is, rather, discovered and applied. Blackstone, the
great authority on the common law, describes judges as "the depositories of
the law, the living oracles" and when they change their positions on legal
questions he states, "but even in such cases, the subsequent judges do not
pretend to make a new law . . . it is declared, not that a sentence was bad law,
but that it was not law."[13] According to this view, man does not take an
active role in formulating rules by which society must exist; his function is
merely to discover and abide by these rules, not create them. In short, the law
preexists man's comprehension of its presence.

A fundamental conflict exists between this notion of law and attempts by
legislatures in the late nineteenth century to combat the growing industrial
abuses. In the common law tradition, statutory law is superfluous, except as
it carries out the function of applying the general principles of the common
law to specific issues. Roscoe Pound expressed concern over this clash:

> The professional feeling that there ought to be little or no legislation on
> legal subjects, the attitude of resentment toward legislation on the part of
> the bench and bar that has led so often to the failure of legislative attempts
> to simplify procedure and has made so much of the labor of social workers
> nugatory after they have put it upon our statute books . . . .[14]

Thus, the courts of the day resisted attempts by men to "make law" when law could not be made by men and consequently overturned legislative attempts to control private employment agencies.

The resistance of the courts to social legislation based upon notions of natural law was reenforced by the appearance in the mid-nineteenth century of the concept of natural evolution, systematized in the writings of Charles Darwin. Adopted from Darwin's biological model of evolution came the concept of social Darwinism. Social Darwinists ardently opposed the enactment of social legislation to curb industrial abuses.

One social Darwinist, Herbert Spencer, was the most forceful foe of legislative attempts to protect misfortunates. In his dynamic book *Social Statics*, he writes:

> The whole effort of nature is to get rid of such, to clear the world of them, and make room for the better . . . if they are sufficiently complete to live, they do live, and it is well that they should live. If they are not sufficiently complete to live, they die and it is best they should.[15]

According to social Darwinism, the legislature, by introducing social legislation to help the poor survive, was interfering with nature's process of elimination of the unfit. Interference with this process was a violation of nature and natural law. Another social Darwinist, William Sumner, states in his appropriately titled book, *What the Social Classes Owe Each Other*:

> The governmental interference can only cause harm . . . we have inherited a vast number of social ills which never came from Nature. They are the complicated products of all the tinkering, muddling and blundering of social doctors in the past . . . .[16]

Thus, the natural law concept and a particular social philosophy combined to halt legislative attempts to regulate private employment agencies specifically and to alleviate the grave social and economic problems which increasingly gripped the nation with increasing industrialization and urbanization in general.

Another judicial obstacle to governmental regulation of private employment agencies stemmed from application of the "due process" clause of the Fourteenth Amendment of the Constitution—an amendment aimed at protecting the rights of newly freed Negro slaves. Social legislation was deemed to be in violation of the provision, "nor shall any state deprive any person of life, liberty or property without due process of law . . . ." A business enterprise and profits therefrom were regarded as *property*, and any regulation of the relationship of employees and employers, or any attempt to regulate amount of profit, was regarded as violation of this amendment. Ironically, the Fourteenth Amendment became the instrument for business exploitation of "industrial wage slaves," at the hands of private employment agents, as well as protection of newly freed Negro slaves.[17]

Repeatedly, courts resisted the legislative attempts to curb social problems through regulation of business practices. For example, Justice Peckham stated in a 1907 New York case dealing with limited working hours in factories for women:

> the tendency of legislatures, in the form of regulatory measures, to interfere with the lawful pursuits of citizens is becoming a marked one in this country and it behooves the court, firmly and fearlessly, to interpose the barriers of their judgments, when invoked to protest against legislative acts . . . .[18]

In another case within the same decade involving maximum working hours, the U.S. Supreme Court held such legislation to be unconstitutional and stated:

> Statutes of the nature of that under review limiting the hours in which grown and intelligent men may labor to earn their living are mere meddlesome interferences with the rights of the individual.[19]

In short, we see that the attempts of the legislatures to find some sort of regulation over private employment agencies and other private enterprises were halted by the conservative stance of the courts toward social legislation. It is against this background of judicial hostility toward legislative interference with business activities that we must understand the development of governmental regulation upon the activities of private employment agencies in the United States. With this in mind, we turn now to an examination of specific case and statutory law.

Specific Case and Statutory Law

Having taken appropriate notice of the need for effective governmental intervention into the internal affairs of the private employment agencies, the legislative bodies of a number of states began to entangle their private agencies in a web of legal restraints. Still, these efforts met with distinctly hostile reaction from the nation's judicial bodies on virtually every level, from state courts to the highest court in the land.

One of the first reported appellate decisions raising the question of the constitutionality of state legislation regulating the practice of private employment agencies took place in California in 1904. In *Ex Parte Dicky*, the California Supreme Court took note of the greatly expanded application of legislation designed to regulate business practices under the police power of the state. The court stated:

> it (the police power) doubtless has been greatly expanded in application during the past century owing to an enormous increase in the number of occupations which are dangerous or so far detrimental to the health of employees as to demand special precautions for their well-being and protection . . . .[20]

However, while the court in *Dicky* recognized that the state might properly, in the exercise of its police power to promote the general welfare of the public, interfere with an individual's pursuit of an occupation, the court concluded that this power was limited to the preservation of the public health, safety and morals. Regulation of private employment agencies was not considered to fall within the permissible scope of the state's power because, "the business (private employment agencies) is . . . not only innocent and innocuous, but is highly beneficial as tending the more quickly to secure labor for unemployed."[21]

Despite the widespread public sentiment that the private employment agency industry needed governmental regulation, the court took the position:

> There is nothing in the nature of the business . . . that in any way threatens or endangers public health, safety or morals. Nor, indeed, is the purpose of this statute to regulate in these regards or in any of them. The declared purpose and the plain effort . . . is to limit the right of an employment agent in making contracts—a right free to those who follow other vocations and arbitrarily to fix compensation which he may receive for the services he renders.[22]

The essence of the California court's position is perhaps best understood by the preceding passage—the concern of the court with interference in the right of contract. This position represents an elevation of contractual rights over the justifiable concern of the legislature for the welfare of members of the public who are dependent upon using these agencies to secure employment. A similar interpretation was echoed in many other court decisions at that time, wherein social legislation designed to regulate the conditions under which men work was struck down by the courts as an unconstitutional violation of contractual rights. With precisely this same reasoning, the courts refused to permit legislatures to tamper with child labor laws, minimum wage laws, maximum working hours, workmen's compensation laws and collective bargaining agreements. Adventures of the legislatures into these areas for the purpose of protecting those in less advantageous bargaining positions was deemed by the judiciary to constitute forbidden intrusions into employer's freedom of contract and, hence, a violation of those property rights protected by the Fourteenth Amendment to the U.S. Constitution.

The great distance traveled by the judiciary in its attitude toward social legislation is best expressed by the further reasoning of the court in *Dicky*. After all, the court pointed out, if employment agencies are to be regulated by the government, then "why should not the butcher and the baker dealing with the necessities of life be restricted in their right of contract and consequently in their profits to ten, five or one percent."[23] What was almost unthinkable to these early jurists is commonplace today. The butcher and the baker's activities, materials, prices and profits are subject to regulation by officers of the government at city, county, state and federal levels. Today virtually every facet of commerce and business comes under some sort of governmental regulation.

While the majority in *Dicky* regarded the California legislature's attempt at regulation of the private employment agencies with much hostility, a dissenting opinion by Justice Shaw recognized that the police power of the state embraced "the preservation and promotion of the general welfare."[24] He stated in unequivocable terms that the circumstances supported the justifiable interference of the state into the operation of employment agencies:

The people can usually be trusted to look after the preservation of their own health in their own way. But owing to their necessitous circumstances, they are sometimes unable to do so properly and in such instances, the legislature has the power to determine for them what shall be done for that purpose. So, also, people may generally be depended upon to make such contracts as their several interests demand and under all ordinary conditions, the right freely to do this cannot be interfered with or controlled by legislative power.

But under some circumstances, a class of persons may be so situated with respect to another class that they are subject to oppression and, though nominally free and at liberty to do as they please, they are in reality compelled to act at dictation of others whose self-interest leads them to take undue advantage and in such case, the legislature may, in the exercise of police power, declare that certain contracts which in its judgment, it deems injurious to general welfare and prosperity of the people, shall not be made and if made, shall not be enforceable.[25]

The following year (1905), the highest court in the city of New York, the Superior Court, upheld a state statute which required a private employment agency to obtain a $25.00 license from the mayor of New York.[26] The court in *People Ex rel Armstrong v. Warden* took the position that an individual has the right to carry on any lawful business or earn his living in any lawful way and that the legislature had no right to interfere with his freedom of action. However, the court went on to state that all businesses and occupations are conducted subject to the exercise of the police power of the state, and a statute promulgated under this police power of the state designed to promote the public health, safety, morals and general welfare must be upheld. In such instances, the court noted, individual freedom must yield to the public good. In this particular situation, the New York court felt that:

> the legislature had the right to take notice agencies are places where emigrants and ignorant people frequently resort to obtain jobs. This relationship affords great opportunities for fraud and oppression and the statute is designed to prevent the same.[27]

The *Armstrong* case set an important precedent: that a state might regulate the conduct of private employment agencies to the extent of screening persons operating these agencies by requiring the licensing of the agency. It was not until ten years later, however, that the United States Supreme Court conclusively decided that employment agencies would be subject to licensing and other regulation by the state governments.

In *Brazee v. Michigan* (1916), the Supreme Court upheld the conviction of an employment agent for sending a job applicant to an employer who had not requested any employees, in violation of the provisions of Act 301, Public Acts of Michigan, 1913.[28] The employment agent sought a reversal of his conviction on the grounds that the licensing of private employment agents and other regulatory provisions of Act 301 was unconstitutional. He claimed that such legislation abridged an individual's right and liberty to contract, and, thereby, constituted a denial of due process of law under the Fourteenth Amendment to the U.S. Constitution. The Supreme Court, noting that under recent decisions similar regulation in other industries had been upheld, stated:

> it is clear that without violating the Federal Constitution, a state may in exercising its police power, require a license for employment agencies and prescribe reasonable regulation . . .the general nature of the business (private employment agencies) is such that unless regulated, many persons may be exposed to misfortunes against which the legislature can properly protect them.[29]

The *Brazee* case clearly established the premise that private employment agencies could be subject to governmental regulation and control. The extent to which the government might exert that control was, however, to be the subject of much litigation in the following years.

Prohibition or Regulation: The Washington Approach

While the Michigan legislature in the *Brazee* case had merely sought the licensing and limited regulation of the activities of private employment agencies, the people of the state of Washington took the matter of private employment agencies into their own hands. They attempted to eliminate effectively the private employment problem altogether by means of a popular initiative measure.

The problems generated by the private employment agencies were particularly acute in the state of Washington. The unstable industry in that area created a large market for short-term, casual labor. This provided a particularly vulnerable field for the exploitation of job-seekers by agents trading in human labor. During the 15 years prior to the initiative attempt, there had been much experimentation with regulating the practices of these private employment agencies, through both direct and indirect controls. The results of these attempts to restrain the agencies from exploiting the casual workers had not been satisfactory, and the abuses by the agents continued. The situation became so serious that the voters of Washington had concluded the only solution to what appeared to be inherent and irradicable evils within the private employment agency industry was a complete prohibition against charging fees to employees for finding them positions. The initiative began with the statement, ''The Welfare of the State of Washington depends upon the welfare of its workers and demands that they be protected from conditions that result in their being liable to imposition and extortion.''[30]

The initiative measure, which eventually passed, would have prohibited private employment agencies from collecting fees from job applicants. Even though the proponents of the Washington initiative argued that it did not completely prohibit employment agencies, since they were still free to seek recompense for their services from the employers, the agents logically regarded the statute as an attempt to drive them out of the state of Washington. This could have been a detrimental precedent, which may have led other states to do likewise. Consequently, the agents gathered together legal funds and turned to the courts for assistance.

Despite broad public sentiment in Washington against private employment agencies, the U.S. Supreme Court determined that the measure was unconstitutional. The Court, in *Adams v. Tanner*,[31] reaffirmed its position in *Brozee*[32] that private employment agencies could be subjected to governmental regulation. However, the court noted that "there is nothing inherently immoral or dangerous to public welfare in acting as the paid representative of another to find a position in which he can earn an honest living. On the contrary, such service is useful, commendable and in great demand."[33] The Court distinguished between the need for regulation of a business and the right to legislate for the abolition of a lawful enterprise.:

> Because abuses may, and probably do, grow up in connection with this business is adequate reason for hedging it about by proper regulations. But this is not enough to justify destruction of one's right to follow a distinctly useful calling in an upright way. Certainly there is no profession, possibly no business which does not offer peculiar opportunities for reprehensible practices and as to every one of them, no doubt, some can be found quite ready earnestly to maintain that its suppression would be in the public interest.[34]

The Court concluded that the initiative measure was arbitrary and oppressive, and it unduly restricted the employment agency's liberty guaranteed by the Fourteenth Amendment to engage in a useful business. The decision in *Adams v. Tanner* was an extremely narrow four-to-five division, with the weight of Justices Brandeis, Holmes, Clark and McKenna in favor of upholding the initiative measure as a valid exercise of the police power to promote the general welfare. Brandeis's carefully written dissenting opinion analyzed in detail the variety of abuses perpetrated by the employment agencies which had led the people of Washington to determine that the only solution to the problems created by the operation of the private employment agencies was this harsh initiative. Brandeis concluded that the people of Washington had ample reason to believe that the general welfare of that state could be preserved only by abolition of private employment agencies:

> There is reason to believe that the people of Washington not only considered the collection by the private employment offices of fees from employees a social injustice, but that they considered the elimination of the practice a necessary preliminary to the establishment of a constructive policy for dealing with the subject of unemployment.[35]

If the philosophy permitting legislatures much freedom to experiment as expounded by Brandeis and Holmes prevailed at this stage, as history shows it did at a later date, then the development and spread of private employment agencies might have been cut off in the United States in 1916. The abuses and public sentiment against these agencies was at such a peak during this period that the Washington legislation might easily have swept the country, if only the Supreme Court had sustained that initiative.

A few years later in 1919, the State of Idaho made a similar attempt to rid itself of private employment agencies.[36] The pendulum of social legislation, however, had not yet begun to swing back. Thus, by the time similar social legislation became acceptable to the judiciary, alternative means of regulating private employment agencies had proved relatively successful in at least masking the more flagrant abuses. In addition, the private employment agency had firmly established itself within the American economy to the extent that complete prohibition was never again seriously considered as a means of correcting the problems generated by the industry. Other varieties of regulation, however, emerged.

Other Direct Regulations

While the *Adams v. Tanner* decision conclusively determined that the private employment agency would remain a part of the American labor landscape, there was little further dispute over the basic right of legislatures to impose some form of regulation upon the industry. As one court stated in 1925:

> it is common knowledge that the business of employment agencies is one dealing with a great body of our own population both native and foreign born which is susceptiable to imposition, deception, and immoral influences. Embracing as it does male, and female, the ignorant, the poor, the young as well as old, the weak and the strong, it would seem to be appropriate that the state should regard them as peculiarly situated for exercise of its protecting arm. It is not an infringment of any right that the legislature has prescribed that he who engages in the business of employment agencies should submit to reasonable regulation.[37]

Interestingly, the courts at an earlier date held that regulation of the fees charged by agencies to applicants was not a reasonable means of regulation and attempts at such regulation were held invalid.

In 1928 the U.S. Supreme Court held in *Ribnick v. McBride* that an employment agency could not be refused a license on the grounds that the fees it charged were exhorbitant.[38] Despite the facts that a major source of the problems generated by the private employment agencies was the charging of exhorbitant and outrageous fees during times of business depression and that 21 states[39] had chosen to meet these problems by statutes regulating the fees charged by the agencies, the Supreme Court made a distinction between fee regulation and other forms of regulation of business. It held that only particular businesses affected with what was termed a ''public interest'' (i.e., public utilities, common carriers) could be subjected to fee regulation.

Justice Stone, in his dissenting opinion, argued that private employment agencies should be subjected to fee regulation on the grounds that the test of what constitutes a business affected with public interest should be, ''Whenever any combination of circumstances seriously curtails the regulative force of competition so that buyers and sellers are placed at such disadvantage in the bargaining struggle that a legislature might reasonably anticipate serious consequences to the community as a whole.''[40] Under this test, the employment agency plays an integral role in the employment-unemployment cycle, which has a profound effect upon great numbers of workers and the economy in general. Some people with whom the employment agent deals are manifestly under economic compulsion to accept the terms dictated by the employment agency. The combination of economic compulsion and grave importance to the well-being of the community as a whole was sufficient in Justice Stone's view to justify fee regulation.

There was sufficient evidence to support the conclusion that the ordinary forces of competition were powerless to prevent or remedy the situation because little capital was needed to open an office and clients were constantly new.[41] Finally, the dissenting opinion noted that there was no valid distinction between price regulation and other forms of regulation, where the former is an appropriate and effective remedy to the evils presented. If particular business conditions demand governmental regulation in order to protect the general welfare, then the most effective means of regulation should be employed.

The court's decision in *Ribnick* was severely criticized in leading legal periodicals, and did not survive for more than a single decade.[42] In 1938 the New York Supreme Court upheld a statute setting maximum fees which employment agencies might charge applicants. The court noted that the applicant ''was out of work and undergoing physical deprivation and mental concern for self and dependents, and had little or no ability to bargain (with the agency) for a price.''[43] In view of these circumstances which characterized a large portion of those persons using employment agencies, the court stated:

In times of depression, the public has a particular interest that the unemployed in seeking employment are not subjected to extortionate charges. Unparalleled demands for relief are made upon the public funds. When a choice is open between accepting public relief or paying extortionate charges, many are likely to go on public relief. Unfortunately, many others who are conscientious and ambitious will take any employment offered even at extortionate charges rather than accept public relief. These considerations render maximum charges a reasonable regulation.[44]

Thus, a concern with the welfare of the public treasury coupled with the fact that the nation had passed through the Great Depression resulted in a judicial consensus that regulation of the fees charged by employment agencies was essential and reasonable regulation. The Supreme Court in *Olsen v. Nebraska* (1941) conclusively determined the issue by an outright reversal of the *Ribnick* decision.[45]

Justice William O. Douglas wrote the majority opinion in *Olsen* and stated that the drift away from the 1928 *Ribnick* holding and its underlying philosophy was so great that it could no longer be considered controlling. Justice Douglas reiterated the admonition that the wisdom of legislation is not an issue for the courts, that differences of opinion over the wisdom of particular pieces of legislation suggest that the choice "should be left where . . .it was left by the Constitution—to the states and to Congress."[46] The only arguments which the opponents of the fee regulation could put forth, Justice Douglas noted, were notions of public policy that were embedded in earlier decisions but which, as Justices Holmes and Brandeis had long warned, should not be read into the Constitution so that such legislation might fall under the brand of "unconstitutionality." Since such notions of public policy "do not find expression in the Constitution, we cannot give them continuing vitality as standards by which constitutionality of economic and social programs of states are determined."[47] The Court, then, returned to the legislatures the power to determine whether fee regulation was an appropriate and necessary means of regulating the private employment agency industry.

Another type of regulation which came under much attack by private employment agencies was the requirement that fees charged to applicants be contingent upon successful placement of the applicant in a job. Prior to such legislation, it was commonplace for agents to collect a fee and make only feeble, if any, effort to place the applicant. The courts did not have much difficulty in sustaining this type of regulation.[48] In *National Employment v. Geraghty* (1932), a federal court stated:

employees . . . have a bargaining power in general far weaker than that of employers. They are often as in these very times, in a desperately poor condition, ready to pay almost anything possible in hope of securing employment. Under such circumstances it is easy to delude them by false hopes and to get their money where there is little or no chance of doing them any service.

Requiring success in placing the applicant not only prevents much fraud and oppression, but benefits a class both needy and numerous . . . also stimulates activity and diligence of the agent.[49]

The ensuing years have generated a wide array of regulations restricting the activities of employment agencies, ranging from the records kept to modes of advertising.[50] Such legislation has been sustained by the judiciary in virtually every instance.

The development of legal restraints upon the operation of private employment agencies has undergone tremendous changes since the early judicial antagonism toward legislative interference with business activity in virtually every form. At several stages of the development of these regulations, the courts have admonished legislative interference with the exercise of property rights by individuals. Gradually, however, the courts recognized the maxim that "when one becomes a member of society he necessarily parts with some rights or privileges which, as an individual not affected by his relation to others he might retain . . . ."[51] Accordingly, infringement of an individual's property rights in his business have yielded to the necessity of regulation for the promotion of the general welfare and prosperity.

The expanded power of the state under its "police power" to protect and promote the general welfare has been recognized not only in the field of the private employment agencies, but in virtually every other sphere of economic activity that touches upon the nations's well-being.

The complaint of the particular business being regulated has frequently been that the overreaching of a few does not justify control of an entire industry. The answer to this challenge is provided in a 1906 article in *Charities and the Commons*:

It is no argument to say that a majority of the persons engaged in a given occupation require no regulation or control. It is enough that a very small minority practice evil and that there exist opportunities for fraud, imposition and immorality. The test is not whether some agencies are properly conducted but whether the business itself is of such a nature that it affords exceptional opportunities for frauds or immoral practices peculiarly affecting the public.[52]

The private employment agency, as we have seen, dealing with individuals in highly precarious financial straits with little bargaining power, is peculiarly vulnerable to abusive practices.

Without sufficient control, the private employment agency may continue to practice almost precisely the same abuses which it engaged in over half a century ago. For instance, examination of the record of the hearings held by

Senator Wayne Morse in 1962 in connection with a bill sponsored by the
senator reveals the "shocking examples of some private employment agency
operators bilking job seekers" in the District of Columbia, which lacked
sufficient regulation of agency operations.[53] Many of the practices cited in
Senator Morse's investigations have changed minutely since their appearance in the late nineteenth century. These practices include:(1) sending
groups of applicants who have already paid registration fees to fictitious
addresses; (2) fee-splitting; (3) dismissals as soon as the applicant has paid
the agent's fee; (4) outrageously high, nonrefundable registration fees and
placement fees.[54] Even more interesting is the continued assertion by the
agents that the industry can police itself to eliminate any abuse without
further regulation.

Indirect Social Control:
Rise of the Public Employment Agency

In the social context of mounting public pressure for greater governmental
control of private employment agencies and the judicial reluctance to permit
it, there developed a movement to establish public employment agencies.
The proponents for establishing these argued that the best way to control the
abuses of the private agencies was to provide free, competitive employment
services.[55]

The social reformers who pushed for the development of public employment services as a means of indirect social control were following in the
moral footsteps of middle and late nineteenth century reformers who made
the exploitation of labor a focal point for sociolegal change.[56] For example,
one of the recognized leaders of the public employment agency movement,
William M. Leiserson, has described the socially accepted theoretical basis
for establishing public agencies. Note the moral tone of his statement made
in 1914:

> In theory, there were designed to furnish clearing houses for labor, to
> bring work and the worker together with the least delay, and to eliminate
> the private labor agent, whose activity as middleman is so often accom-
> panied by fraud, misrepresentation and extortion.[57]

The moral movement to establish public employment agencies generated
a major philosophical struggle over whether or not the government should
compete with private enterprise in the employment services field or in any
other field. Public officials debated the issue before making a decision to set
up public employment services. The Massachusetts Commission to Investi-

gate Employment Offices states, in 1911, the standard argument against public employment agencies:

> For well-known reasons we never think of establishing governmental grocery stores and governmental dry goods shops in the hope of having the community better served than by private enterprise. The same reasons should clearly govern our attitude toward employment offices, unless it is shown that the employment office business is different from other business.[58]

The philosophical struggle was resolved in favor of growing public opinion that "generally held that neither employers nor workers should have to pay for assistance in the employment process that was so vital to the economic welfare of all citizens."[59] Thus, the public employment agency concept became associated with the more general concept of government's responsibility to promote the general public welfare by providing "life essential" services. In this sense, the creation of public employment agencies represents an expansion of citizenship rights to include employment assistance.

Municipal governments made the first attempts to provide free employment services. The first known experiment was conducted by New York City in 1834. At that time, New York City was deluged by problems associated with the influx of immigrants, who needed work. The private agencies could not adequately handle the supply of job-seekers, and numerous incidents of abuses came to the attention of the city officials and concerned social reformers. For similar reasons, San Francisco in 1868 established a public employment service. Nine other cities followed suit at the turn of the century.[60] Municipal employment offices soon gave way to state-run employment offices, largely as a logical response to the need for greater administrative coordination. And, in 1933, employment services as a right of citizenship, along with a host of other work-related rights, were formalized on the federal level by the passage of the Wagner-Peyser Act.

Private v. Public Employment Agency

The ability of public employment agencies to compete successfully with private agencies, and thereby indirectly control them, has been limited. The limited extent of indirect control can be understood within the context of an evolving public bureaucracy whose general history could be characterized by lack of cogent administrative principles, inaccurate data gathering and insufficient information exchange between organizational units. In addition, the evolution of public bureaucracies has been politically determined.[61] Public bureaucracy is subject to alternations in scope and direction with each succeeding political administration; the political nature of public employment agencies has resulted in much fluctuation in structure and procedure between and within states, which further limited the ability of the public agencies to compete with the private. In some instances, competition is limited by design. For example, it is a common practice in many states to select the head of the public employment service system from among executives and owners of the private employment agencies. This practice almost insures that the public employment service will not develop into a viable competitor of the private agencies. The political activities of the National Employment Association, which claims to represent over 1,500 private employment agencies, have served to "limit potential competition from public agencies."[62] The NEA has lobbied to limit the U.S. Employment Service applicants to "blue-collar workers, including the poor and the disadvantaged."[63]

Thus, competition between public and private agencies has been generally limited to a certain class of workers. From its inception, the public agency has tended to concentrate its efforts upon citizen-clients with the least value in the human marketplace. The private agencies, in contrast, have been continuously shifting their clientele upwards, favoring the growing white-collar market. In order to understand better this and other differences between private and public employment agencies today, it would be useful to examine some of the data gathered by the Institute of Industrial Relations at the University of California, Berkeley. In 1968, the institute published a report on a survey of placement and counseling among private and public employment agencies in the San Francisco Bay Area.[64] I have been in touch with the project director, Dr. Margaret Thal-Larsen, since the beginning of the survey. Her findings provide some useful insight into the nature of the differences between private and public employment agencies.

The first notable difference between public and private employment agencies in Thal-Larsen's stratified sample regards services offered. Both public and private agencies offer specialized services, but the nature and extent of specialization vary considerably. Typically, public agencies tend to specialize infrequently, but when they do it is according to the socio-economic characteristics of the applicant-clientele. In contrast, private agencies are frequently specialized along occupational lines rather than according to any characteristics of the applicant-clientele. This is indicated by the data in Table 5. A majority of the public agencies in the institute's sample (56 percent, N = 16) were not specialized. Of those public agencies that were specialized (44 percent), they tended to specialize according to the age of the clientele and his residence. Among private agencies in the sample, the overwhelming majority (73 percent, N = 30) were specialized. All 73

TABLE 5
Specialization of Public and Private Employment Agencies
By Occupation and Worker Characteristic
in San Francisco Bay Area
(in percent)

Specialization	Type of Agency	
	Public	Private
No Specialization	56.3	26.7
Specialized	43.7	73.3
By Occupation	12.5	73.3
White-collar (all, or most occupations)	6.3	50.0
White-collar, primarily professional,		
Technical and managerial	—	6.7
White-collar, primarily clerical	—	3.3
Blue-collar, (or most occupations)	6.2	3.3
Domestics	—	3.3
Other occupations	—	6.7
By Worker Characteristic	31.2	—
Age—16 to 22	18.7	—
Resident of poverty area	12.5	—
N (=100%)	16	30

Source: Margaret Thal-Larsen, *Placement and Counseling in a Changing Labor Market: Public and Private Employment Agencies and Schools* (Berkeley: Institute of Industrial Relations, 1970), p. 106a.

percent were specialized by occupational category. The most common occupational category was white collar.

The first difference suggests much about the separate organizational missions of public and private agency. Very simply, private agencies structure their activities for processing those members of the human marketplace who are the most marketable. The greatest manpower need in the world in which we live is for white-collar workers. Profit-seeking private agencies logically choose to concentrate their efforts on placing white-collar workers. Nonprofit public agencies are aimed to serve the much less marketable members, and, therefore, do not specialize in white-collar workers.

The services provided by public agencies differ markedly from those provided by private agencies. As indicated by the data in Table 6, public agencies provide a wider variety of services. The managers of both types of agencies in the sample overwhelmingly mentioned "counseling" as a service their agency provides to applicants. (The nature of the counseling is critical, and it is examined more fully in chapter 5.) The definition of counseling, however, varied considerably, according to Dr. Thal-Larsen:

In the private as in the public agencies the variations as to what was regarded as counseling were very wide indeed. And in both types of agencies, its content reflected variations in the needs of the individual

TABLE 6
Services Other Than Placement Offered to Job Applicants
By Private and Public Employment Agencies
In the San Francisco Bay Area
(in percent)

Services Offered	Type of Agency	
	Public	Private
Counseling	75.0	90.0
Testing	62.5	63.3
Labor Market Information	31.3	—
"Employability Development"	31.3	—
"Outreach"	31.3	—
Work Incentive Program	25.0	—
Referral to Health or Psychiatric services	25.0	—
Petty Cash, clothes	18.8	—
Referral to Training	12.5	—
Resume Preparation	—	23.3
Provide office equipment for practice	—	13.3
Other Services*	18.8	—
No service other than placement offered	—	10
N (=100%)	16	30

*Other services include: referral to Travelers' Aid, CEP or to "all supportive services that can be imagined.

Note: will not add to 100 percent, since most respondents gave more than one answer.

Source: Thal-Larsen, *Placement and Counseling*, p. 148.

---

office's clientele. Some private agency respondents saw employment counseling primarily as a matter of advising their numerous young applicants for clerical jobs about the correct use of cosmetics, the "right" clothes to wear in their job search, and the particular and often peculiar preferences of the employers to whom they were being referred. But as often, this counseling included a great deal of detailed information concerning the local job market and it might rest upon interest, aptitude and performance testing, which was extensively given in these offices. Particularly in the case of entrant and reentrant workers, there was evidence that real assistance was often given in making a vocational choice.[65]

The private agency combines counseling and placement into one task, whereas the public agency does not. The applicants to the public agencies are defined by managers and staff as generally in great need of supportive services before they could be considered job-ready. The applicants processed by private agencies are generally much more job-ready, in need of only minor supportive services.

TABLE 7
Type of Service Received By 19,996 Applicants
From Public and Private Employment Agencies, July 1968
In San Francisco Bay Area
(in percent)

Type of Service Received	Type of Agency	
	Public	Private
Referred to Employer for Job	29.7	75.6
Referred to Training	4.9	1.4
Referred to Another Agency for Service other than Training	6.8	4.7
Given Service other than Job Referral (including counseling)	53.6	13.0
No Service Given	5.0	5.3
N (=100%)	15,052	4,944

Source: Thal-Larsen, *Placement and Counseling*, p. 383.

A third area of comparison regards the type of service that applicants actually receive from private and public agencies. Typically, the private employment agency admits to making no particular efforts to increase the employability of only marginally placeable applicants, whereas the public employment agency claims to make every possible effort to develop the employability of the applicant. One manager of a public agency (Youth Opportunity Center) in Thal-Larsen's sample elaborated on such efforts:

> We have group talks, show them movies, discuss grooming, get them free haircuts, hairdos, clothes. We coach them on filling out applications, how to conduct themselves in employer interviews, how to take tests . . . .[66]

To the job-seeker, meaningful employment service means getting a job. On this measure, private employment agencies seem to outperform the public agencies. The data in Table 7 suggest that the chances of receiving a job referral are more than two times greater at a private agency than at a public agency. The 20.7 percent of the public agency applicants who were referred to an employer for a job might possibly have received a similar referral had they gone to a private agency. However, it is very unlikely that the majority of public agency applicants who received a service other than job referral would have received any service from a private agency, much less a job referral. The private employment agency, which I studied as a participant observer, would unceremoniously inform those applicants who were valued lowly by the human marketplace the cold facts of life, ''Sorry, but we only work with professional people,'' or, ''Sorry, we do not handle wage earners.''

In terms of my limited interest in trying to ascertain the extent to which the public employment agencies have functioned to control indirectly the private employment agencies, what can be concluded thus far? The idea of providing a free, competitive public employment service appears to have been only partially realized. In general, public agencies do not appear to compete with private agencies. Private agencies process a different clientele, mostly white-collar workers. The main way in which public employment agencies have functioned as indirect controls is through eliminating the exploitive private agency that thrives upon disadvantaged members of the human marketplace by providing free employment services.

Public employment agencies have not been immune to criticism for their treatment of applicants. In fact, the mass treatment offered by the public agencies has probably discouraged highly valued members of the human marketplace from becoming applicants. Some interesting experiments aimed to improve the relationship between public employment agent and applicant have taken place.

Today, a number of government-funded manpower programs provide additional free employment services to economically depressed people (e.g., WIN, Project SER). Each program represents an extension of the concept that people need and should have free employment services as a right of citizenship. In their own way, each program acts as an indirect control over the abuses suffered by people at the hands of the private employment agent at a time when the private sector held a monopoly over employment services.

The movement to effect social control over the activities of private employment agents generated a complex set of conflicting social concepts of a philosophical, political and sociological nature. The resolution of some of these conceptual conflicts earmarked areas of significant social change, especially in the area of governmental regulation of private enterprise.

The desire for social control over the problem of exploitation of the disadvantaged and least significant members of the human marketplace was so great and in light of the failure to obtain significant direct social control of the private employment agents, an indirect form of social control was set up by the federal and state governments. Free, public employment agencies were established; thereby extending the rights of citizenship to include free employment agency services.

NOTES

1. 38 *Yale Law Journal* 225 (December 1928).
2. See chapter 2 for an extensive discussion of the wide variety of abusive practices that have frequented the private employment industry.

3. Adams v. Tanner, 244 U.S. 590, 605 (1916) (Brandeis, J., dissenting).

4. Ibid.

5. 38 *Yale Law Journal*.

6. 14 *Cornell Law Quarterly* 75 (December 1928).

7. Quoted in Adams v. Tanner, *supra* at 604.

8. Ibid.

9. Ibid., 612.

10. Ibid., 604.

11. 15 *American Bar Association Journal* 57 (Fall 1929).

12. Jerome Hall, *Theft, Law and Society* (Indianapolis: Bobbs-Merrill, 1935), p. 3.

13. Fred V. Cahill, Jr., *Judicial Legislation* (New York: Ronald Press, 1952), p. 9.

14. Roscoe Pound, *The Spirit of the Common Law* (Cambridge, Mass.: Jones, 1921), p. 45.

15. Herbert Spencer, *Social Statics* (New York: Appleton, 1864), pp. 414-15.

16. William G. Sumner, *What the Social Classes Owe Each Other* (New Haven: Yale University Press, 1925), p. 118.

17. A.L. Todd, *Justice on Trial* (New York: McGraw-Hill, 1964), p. 9.

18. People v. William, 189 N.Y. 131 (1907).

19. Lockner v. New York, 198 U.S. 45, 53.

20. Ex Parte Dicky, 144 Cal. 234 (1904).

21. Ibid.

22. Ibid.

23. Ibid.

24. Ibid.

25. Ibid.

26. People Ex rel Armstrong v. Warden, 183 N.Y. 223 (1905).

27. Ibid.

28. Brazee v. Michigan, 241 U.S. 340 (1916).

29. Ibid.

30. Adams v. Tanner, *supra*.

31. 244 U.S. 590 (1916).

32. 241 U.S. 246 (1916).

33. Adams v. Tanner, *supra*.

34. Ibid.

35. Ibid.

36. Idaho made a similar unsuccessful attempt at elimination of private employment agencies, see *Idaho Compiled Statutes*, 1919.

37. Clark v. McBride, 101 N.J. 213 (1925).

38. 277 U.S. 350 (1928).

39. See 17 *California Law Review* 55 (November 1928).

40. Ribnick v. McBride, *supra*.

41. Massachusetts Commission to Investigate Employment Offices, 1911, cited in Ribnick v. McBride, *supra* (dissenting opinion).

42. For example, see 42 *Harvard Law Review* 126 (November 1928); 17 *California Law Review* 55 (November 1928); 28 *Columbia Law Review* 970 (November

1928); 14 *Cornell Law Quarterly* 75 (December 1928); 7 *North Carolina Law Review* 81 (December 1928).

43. 2 New York Supp 2nd 947 (1938).

44. Ibid.

45. Olsen v. Nebraska, 313 U.S. 236 (1941).

46. Ibid.

47. Ibid.

48. For a discussion of contingent fee regulations, see 32 *Columbia Law Review* 1235 (November 1932); 46 *Harvard Law Review* 328 (December 1932); 18 *Cornell Law Review* 118 (December 1932).

49. National Employment Exchange v. Geraghty 60 F. 2d 2nd 918 (1932).

50. For example, Sales Consultants, Inc. v. DiCarlo, 24 App. 2d 747, 263 N.Y.S. 2nd 561 (name); Business Management v. Dept. of Industrial Relations, 26 Cal 2d 26 (location); Freedman v. O'Connell, 5 App. Div 2nd 858, 172 N.Y.S. 2nd 455 (advertising); Roslyn Employment Agency v. Ryan 234 N.Y.S. 2d 79 (records); Smith v. Arywilz, 193 Cal App. 2d 844, 15 Cal. Rptr. 418 (form of contracts).

51. Munn v. Illinois, 14 U.S. 133.

52. "The New York Employment Agency Law Upheld," *Charities and the Commons*, February 10, 1906, pp. 678-80.

53. *Congressional Record*, 87th Congress, 2nd Sess., pp. 7773-77.

54. Ibid.

55. See Leonard P. Adams, *The Public Employment Service in Transition, 1933-1968* (Ithaca, N.Y.: Cornell University Press, 1969); William Haber and Daniel H. Kruger, *The Role of the United States Employment Service in a Changing Economy* (Kalamazoo, Michigan: W.E. Upjohn Institute, 1964); and Shelby M. Harrison, *Public Employment Offices* (New York: Russell Sage Foundation, 1924).

56. Haber and Kruger, *Employment Service in a Changing Economy*, p. 23.

57. Ibid., p. 22.

58. Ibid., pp. 23-24.

59. Ibid.

60. Ibid.

61. Reinhard Bendix, *Nation-Building and Citizenship* (New York: Wiley, 1964).

62. Leonard P. Adams, "Employment Agencies: Public vs. Private," *Challenge* 15 (January-February 1967):32.

63. Ibid.

64. Margaret Thal-Larsen, *Placement and Counseling in a Changing Labor Market: Public and Private Employment Agencies and Schools* (Berkeley: Institute of Industrial Relations, 1970).

65. Ibid., p. 155.

66. Ibid.

4

SALESMEN IN
PROFESSIONAL
CLOTHING

Any occupation wishing to exercise professional authority must find a technical basis for it, assert an exclusive jurisdiction, link both skills and jurisdiction to standards of training, and convince the public that its services are uniquely trustworthy.[1]

Harold L. Wilensky

In this chapter we examine the social conditions influencing private employment agents to seek professional status, how they are seeking it and whether or not they are succeeding. Then, an assessment of the overall implications from a public policy standpoint will be rendered.

The Advantages of Professionalization

Why would any occupational group desire professional status?[2] At first blush, professionalization may be considered simply a collective effort by an occupational group to increase its power vis-à-vis other occupations and improve its prestige.[3] It is, after all, supposedly within the nature of an open-class society for everyone with the appropriate skills to have access to the highest status ratings. From the point of view of the private employment agent's occupational association (the National Employment Association) the advantages accrued from professionalization are:

The true professional, because of the service he performs, received from society his *livelihood* and, perhaps as significant, the *respect* of the society for which he has rendered his unique service.[4]

81

This quote is from an article announcing an intensification of NEA efforts to attain professional status for private employment agents through an accreditation program.

Money and prestige are not the only advantages of professional recognition. As the NEA notes in the same article quoted above:

> Society is not equipped to judge the special skills of a professional. It must consider only the results of the professional's application of the skills. *Only the industry of which the professional is a member is qualified to recognize the competence of an individual member in which he applies these skills*. The industry certifies those of its membership who have met certain standards which members of the industry have established as most declarative of professional competence.[5]

NEA fully realizes that it is to its advantage to attain professional status. They find attractive the idea that professionals themselves determine who is and who is not qualified to enter their ranks. Self-control over accreditation is especially important to private employment agencies. Because there are presently few legal restrictions impinging upon private employment agency practices, an agency can be set up quickly and with little capital. The industry is therefore plagued by "fly-by-night" operators who move into an area and make a swift profit by whatever means possible. Often operators are unethical. Because such practices sometimes arouse public outrage through the efforts of a crusading journalist or politician, it is to the advantage of the private employment agency industry to eliminate the fly-by-night operations. Established private employment agencies wish to avoid governmental investigations and legislative attempts to create restrictions on all agencies, which might result from a flurry of unfavorable publicity. There is a real fear among employment agents that if ethical standards of performance were set and enforced by public authorities many of the agents now working might be disqualified. Thus, private employment agents are understandably in a dilemma over control of work standards. Some standards that would screen out blatant crooks are desirable. Up to this time, the dilemma was partially resolved by appeals to professional status. This partial resolution is not without its own advantage. That is, appeals to professional status enable the private employment agencies to pretend to the public that some sort of internal system of professional control is at work.

There is an additional advantage that is a direct result of efforts by private employment agencies to determine the personal qualifications, for their field: competition is limited. In most states, the main requirements to open a private employment agency are a cash bond and a waiting period of six months before it is allowed to work for an agency that rivals the former employing agency. If it was easier to open a private employment agency, the field would be more competitive than it now is.

Legitimation and Public Consensus

A professional is supposed to adhere to the "service ideal," wherein commercial and personal interests are subordinate to the needs of the clients.[6] One private employment agent, whom we interviewed , challenged the relevance of the service ideal as a determinant of professionalism. He correctly pointed out that many "unethical" acts are committed by doctors and attorneys. Still, both groups he mentioned are considered ideal-typical professions. The entrenchment of doctors and attorneys in professional status positions is, however, based not so much on the individual practitioner's ethical conduct but in the public's confidence that long, prescribed technical training will have weeded out those less ethically inclined. The professional training schools consciously attempt to instill within the students a clear idea of what constitutes professional, ethical behavior.[7] In addition to the schools, there is typically an apprenticeship program built into the established professions. Throughout the professional's career, the occupational association has a built-in mechanism for processing any complaints made against him along with the authority to sanction and dismember. It is easy to believe that the established professions can and do exert external and internal forms of control over their practitioners and, perhaps consequently, reduce unethical behavior and promote adherence to the service ideal. Among private employment agents, however, there is no movement to develop nationally required schools that would train agents how to place applicants in the most appropriate jobs (although some of the franchised chain agencies have short schooling sessions to train new owners in how to make money). No comprehensive exams to test an agent's competence are widely used (although new agents are often given a brief written test by the hiring agency). There is also no strong built-in mechanism for processing complaints of unethical behavior (although in many regions the local association leadership does what it can to process complaints, such as talk with the offending agency when public outcry stirs up). Therefore, it is difficult to believe that the practitioner's behavior is sufficiently subject to external and internal control to warrant attribution of the professional service ideal. Private employment agents claim that they too, like the established professions, are service oriented—they offer a service to employers and applicants. Chapter 2 suggested much doubt about compliance to the professional service ideal. Still, the task of private employment agents is to obtain a public consensus on their compliance to it. This means constructing a positive public image of the enterprise. Three psychological techniques are presently employed by agents to shape the public's perception of the business in their favor. They are:

1. "Professional Trappings"—whereby agents grant themselves impressive new job titles and locate their offices in prestigious areas.
2. "Self-Proclamation"—whereby the agents' association issues certificates to its members which supposedly attest the bearer's competence.
3. "From Occupational Association to Profession"—whereby local and national organizations are established primarily for public relations and legislative lobbying.

"Professional Trappings"

There was a time when job middlemen were content to be called "employment agents," but no longer. Today, the minimumly acceptable title preferred is "employment counselor." Many agents prefer different titles, such as "job consultants," "executive recruiters," "professional searchers" or "management consultants." A number of special terms are also used within the industry to designate different types of agencies. A large employment agency, for example, is commonly known as a "body factory." Agencies dealing primarily with lower white- and blue-collar workers are frequently deemed "flesh peddlers." The agencies engaged in extensive searches for a person with specialized skills are called "head hunters." Applicants and employers seldom hear these in-group terms. Yet, agents often use these terms to refer to the manner in which the various agencies go about their everyday business. It is probably peculiar to an occupational group with an inferiority complex that negative status labels for itself and others like itself are a part of its everyday vocabulary.

Many agents seek to disassociate themselves from their counterparts who operated before World War II. Before then, almost all private employment agents operated out of curbside offices or in "dingy" second-floor rooms over saloons and stores. Jobs available through the agency were usually posted on outdoor billboards. Today, a tenth-floor, plushly furnished suite in an attractive office building is a common location for employment agencies. Even the smaller, one- or two-man agencies manage to have offices in shopping centers. The shift in office locations reflects a greater attempt to attract higher status applicants and to project a more successful, professional public image.

"Self-Proclamation"

Proudly displayed on the walls of many private employment agencies are framed certificates bearing a deliberate resemblance to the licenses displayed in doctors' and attorneys' offices. These certificates are inscribed in gold or silver lettering with the impressive titles "Certified Employment Consultant" or "Recommended Employment Counselor" (and, as is the way with impressive titles, for convenience they are abbreviated to E.E.C. and R.E.C.). Ann Palmer Haynes, a Washington, D.C. employment agency owner, testified before a U.S. Senate subcommittee concerning her efforts to find out what authority was behind these certificates. Her testimony is recounted by Malcom Margolin:

> Mrs. Ann Palmer Haynes, owner of a Washington employment agency, told Wayne Morse's committee about her experience with these degrees. One day she received a direct mail circular offering her the honor of competing for her E.E.C. She tried to telephone the American Institute of Employment Counseling only to discover that it had no phone. Further investigation revealed that the organization was not even licensed to do business in Washington.
>
> Mrs. Haynes finally tracked down the elusive Institute by getting in touch with the manager of the building whose address was listed on the Institute's return envelope. All mail for the American Institute of Employment, she learned, was being turned over to a local company, the Graebner Employment Agency. "This type of thing is most misleading," concluded Mrs. Haynes. "What qualifications does the Graebner Employment Agency have to bestow initials of any kind on anyone?" Yet hundreds of status hungry job brokers have acquired these "degrees," and although I would hate to be a spoilsport, I suspect that Mr. Graebner's sheepskin is a bit less valuable than a college education.[8]

The California Employment Agency Association, like many other state employment associations, also issues certificates of competence to its members. According to the California association, to be judged competent enough to place a man in a job which he may have for the rest of his life, an agent must pass a test concerning his familiarity with the state laws governing private employment agencies and a list of ethics. The agent is not required to demonstrate a knowledge of the job market or of vocational guidance. Normally, a new agent can learn in two or three days (or hours) what he needs to know in order to pass the test administered by the CEAA.

On the national level, the National Employment Association recently launched a certification program of its own that is more promising. Whether or not this promise will be met remains to be seen. Included in the procedures for attaining the degree would be an interview by local agency owners and a test administered, but not graded, by a college testing center. The areas in which a "professional" knowledge will be demanded are:

1. Interview principles and techniques
2. Job description and specification
3. Employee selection
4. Placement procedure (recruitment, solicitation and referral)
5. Economic and job market information and sources
6. Aids for applicants
7. Agency management
8. State and national legislation
9. Your state private employment agency law.[9]

Requiring the agents to demonstrate a knowledge of both the job market and aids for applicants is a step forward. Conspicuous by its absence, however, is any examination of the agents' knowledge of vocational guidance. Another point limiting attribution of professional status to the NEA Certification Program is the lack of a guarantee that the program will be stringent enough in examining the agents—who will also be members of the NEA. True professionalization would require that the certification procedure will become neither a rubber stamp nor an oligarchical means of restricting competition. A committee of local agency owners will be among those examining the "testee," and the committee could decide to limit the number of new entries awarded the certificate. Therefore, if the certificates come to have greater value, the examination procedure could clog that circulation of new competitive blood into the private employment agency field. An effective enforcement board might ensure that the testee's knowledge is being put into practice.

"From Occupational Association to Profession"

The circumstances that caused private employment agents to form a national association are noted by Cowgill:

In 1918, at the end of the World War, when the general public was making large demands upon all types of businesses to "cleanse their skirts," a group of employment agents who were interested in the good name and integrity of their business, met in the City of Chicago and organized an association of private employment agencies known as the "National Employment Board." Representatives from large agencies in such cities as New York, Chicago, Cleveland, and San Francisco were present, as well as university professors and chamber of commerce members. The avowed purpose of this organization was to meet the *public criticism*, satisfy the *newspapers* which had demanded that some action be taken if employment agency advertisements were to continue, to *protect the legitimate agencies* against the corruption that had been practiced by some agents during the recent period, *organize standard practices, and to combat adverse legislation*.[10]

The first local private employment agency association was probably formed soon after two agents had opened shop in the same city. A penchant for forming associations seems to be endemic to the occupation, and for several good reasons. They are stated above in the passage from Cowgill, but in reverse order of importance. The prime function of the ubiquitous agency associations on the city, state and national level is to prevent legislatures from outlawing private employment agencies, or from seriously restricting their practices. This function, however, is tempered by a concurrent need to "quiet the howl" of public criticism. A howling public has, upon occasion, aroused the legislature to act—and sometimes overreact. In order to stay on good terms with the legislators and the public watchdogs, visible evidence of a sincere attempt to sanction agents who violate ethics is periodically offered. Often a blatantly corrupt agency or agent that has caught the public eye is publicly disavowed by the agency association.

An early example of the paradoxical role of the employment agencies' association in blocking major regulatory legislation, while at the same time pushing for the prevention of outstanding abuses by their colleagues, is illustrated in Cowgill's study of the Employment Agencies Protective Association of the United States:

For the purpose of meeting legal issues the agencies organized the Employment Agencies Protective Association of the United States. To this association membership is less limited than to the National Employment Board. *This association has questioned the legality of many laws, and has employed one of the best known constitutional lawyers to handle its cases*. In Chicago this association has tried to organize all of the employment agencies of the City. This has been almost an impossible job because of the diversity of interests. Several meetings have been held when something of interest to all of the agencies has been before the state legislature, or the newspapers were making some demand . . . .

The National Association of Employment Agents cooperates with the Chamber of Commerce, and has been instrumental in instituting several important developments in the employment agency business, such as the abolition of the registration fee in 1919. A difficult fight is ahead of any organization whenever it attempts to fulfill the need of adequate legislation. *Few agents desire to be told what they can and cannot do. It is only when they see they must accept regulation to protect themselves, that they will suffer regulation*. Even then several will resist and claim their legal rights. Only by building up public resistance to certain practices can they be abolished. The case of the advance payments is a good example. In the first place it was difficult to see the idea of its abolition to the association. In the second place it was impossible to sell it to the remainder of the employment agents. *Advance payments in certain classes of agencies are rare today, but they are rare because one of Chicago's largest newspapers refused to publish the advertisements of any employment agency charging an advance fee, and the people using the services of the employment agents have resisted the payment of the fee so effectively.*

The private employment agencies are only one group of businesses that have taken measures to improve the ethics of their vocation. As we go back into history we find that nearly every vocation has at one time or another taken these steps. The money lenders in historical days were among the first to take action. In recent times the insurance companies, and real estate brokers have been the outstanding examples. Sometimes the main incentives toward professional regulation are for the purposes of defeating the steps of legislatures, at other times legislatures are requested to aid in abolishing corruption from the vocation, and quite often the association is primarily for the purpose of advertising. *The abolition of registration fees which is the one reform attributed to the national association of private employment agencies, was probably a very minor concession on their part*; for so many states had already regulated its collection so severely that it netted the agencies no gain. In fact it might have been a hindrance, for the agency must either return it or give a thorough accounting of how it was spent.

There is still much to be hoped for in the field of laws regulating private employment agencies, but a beginning has been made, and a few worthy things accomplished.[11]

We have included this lengthy passage verbatim not only because it is an accurate analysis of a "professional" employment agent association not published elsewhere but also more importantly because it provides a historical insight into this type of association as it existed a half a century ago. Thus, perhaps, we can judge the progress that has been made. Cowgill emphasized that although the employment agency association voiced a desire to spearhead the reform movement in their industry, most agents resisted regulation. Only *after* a reform movement began, such as the fight to abolish registration fees, did the employment agency association make grand gestures of reform, which it then claimed to have been pursuing all along.

The National Employment Association is now the major nationwide organization for private employment agencies. The NEA's objective as stated in its by-laws is:

> To promote constructive publicity and to create a better understanding, acquaintance, coordination and cooperation among employment services; to increase the efficiency of the agency service by the promotion of effective methods for serving employers and job applicants, by the consideration of the relations between employers and employees, and by the investigation and study of industrial and economic conditions; to set and maintain the highest standards of practice; to amply protect its members against all acts, methods and practices inimical to the best interests of the service.
>
> To work in close coordination with state and local associations on such matters as public relations and legislation.[12]

The NEA included the promotion of effective service among its objectives; but public relations and legislation, the objectives stated last, seem to be their most active concern. The NEA publication, *Placement Age: The Voice of the Private Placement Industry*, devotes most of its journal to a discussion of pending legislation and to how each agent may and should influence legislation. One article, entitled "It's Too Late Now," urges employment agents "to get to know" their lawmakers before restrictive legislation is passed:

> Don't be reluctant to "educate" your Congressmen and Legislators. As busy men, their entire attitude toward our industry may be formed by one incident, impression, or conversation.
>
> Congressman and State Legislators like to know what affects their constituents. Let them know why we are opposed to the expansion of the United States Employment Services, and to enactment of state placement fee restrictions. Point out that we have favored and testified on behalf of bills aimed at eliminating discriminatory hiring practices, and that we have made great strides in policing our own industry. Let them know of the valuable and efficient service private employment agencies provide in our free enterprise society.[13]

As mentioned above, the NEA is currently crusading to eliminate discriminatory hiring practices, and in every issue of *Placement Age* attention is devoted to this problem. There are striking parallels between this crusade and the crusade of the 1918 Employment Agencies Protective Association to end registration fees. First, in both cases the original impetus came from outside the industry. Second, the association leadership and many of the members appear to want honest reform, but there are many other agents who may be too "greedy" to end their abuses. Third, the association, while championing one reform that the public is already relentlessly demanding, is blocking other reforms. At the present, the NEA is resisting state placement fee restrictions and policing by state and federal regulatory agencies.

The NEA spends large sums to "educate" legislators and others of the importance of private employment agencies and of the importance of leaving them unhampered by external regulation. Occasionally, the methods of the NEA seem to go beyond what could be called education. Margolin presents some evidence from the Morse investigation that clearly suggests that the National Employment Association is sufficiently economically powerful not only to coopt government officials but also to provide well-paying jobs to "cooperative" witnesses:

The NEA's campaign to educate "clear-thinking Americans" runs into a lot of money. In one year alone, the NEA set about raising $163,000 for its war chest, and 3 months later it appealed for another $75,000. And the NEA uses its enormous wealth with a great skill.

Take the way it tried to manipulate Senator Morse's hearings. These hearings were brought about largely because of the statements of William J. Mawhinney of the Washington, D.C., Better Business Bureau, who demanded stricter legislation to stem the flood of complaints pouring into his office. Called to the witness stand, Mr. Mawhinney said he was no longer connected with the Better Business Bureau. He also denied that he had ever made the statements attributed to him. And he opined that the current laws were adequate. Senator Morse was perplexed. But further questioning elicited the fact that Mr. Mawhinney was now an employee of one of the Washington employment agencies being investigated.

The Washington employment agencies also raised special funds. They imported witnesses from all over the country. Their lawyers pleaded for more time to study the situation. But Wayne Morse held firm. His report to the Senate urged strict regulation of the employment agency business. The bill was introduced in 1962. It has been reintroduced for the past 4 years. Each time, the NEA, the U.S. Chamber of Commerce, and the other big-business lobbies have seen its defeat.[14]

In sum, these three propaganda techniques ("Professional Trappings," "Self-Proclamation" and "From Occupational Association to Profession") are used in the hope of producing public myths about the nature of the private employment agency business. The aim of these myths, of course, is to gain profession status legitimation based upon the appearance of public consensus. We turn now away from myth of professionalism and look at the actual activities of the occupation.

What Private Employment Agents Actually Do

The nature of the private employment agency business is essentially sales. Jobs are sold to applicants, and applicants are sold to employers. The business of the agency may not be in obtaining jobs, but obtaining fees; and the counseling process consists in a large part of manipulating the applicant to lower his sense of self-worth (which will be discussed in greater detail in the next chapter), thus making it easier for the agent to place the applicant in a job and collect the fee. The fact is that most private employment agents are hired as species of salesmen, and they are seldom expert in any other role. This is brought out by information gathered during the summer of 1964 when I worked as a licensed private employment agent at a large Midwestern agency doing participant observation research.

The sales process begins with the job opening. A few of these openings are called in by the interested companies—usually the jobs are for some specialists the company is having difficulty in hiring. But the majority of the openings is obtained when the counselors call the companies, ostensibly to stimulate interest in the qualifications of some particular applicants. During the call, the counselor inquires about other possible personnel needs. Here is a sample presentation, used by my agency to teach its counselors how to "sell."

> Sir, my name is _____. I'm with the _____ department of _____ Agency. I don't know what you have open, but I'm calling in regards to a _____ (title of position, like "industrial engineer") who has _____ years of experience, _____ education, and is (married or unmarried). He is presently (employed or unemployed) and available for an interview (give possible time).
>
> If the employer expresses a desire to see the applicant, then obtain the following information: the salary paid for the position and their policy on the fee (who pays, the employer or the applicant?). If the employer does not want to commit himself on the salary, ask him the highest and the lowest he will pay for that position.

Unlike the applicants themselves, counselors looking for openings generally bypass personnel departments, especially in the smaller companies, and go straight to the executives involved. The executives know more about the specific jobs, they do the actual hiring and they do not feel so threatened by employment agencies as do the personnel managers. After all, in theory, if a personnel manager were doing his job properly, employment agencies might not be necessary.

Salesmanship is a skill not everyone has. Yet, it is too general and requires no specific formal training other than the knowledge of the product sold. Almost all private employment agents function not as employment "counselors" but as job-information salesmen. As, one "executive recruiter" stated, "we offer a communications service."

Another agent stated the importance of salesmanship in his job:

I: Were you ever a salesman?

R: Yeah, well, I was a salesman, but the majority of counselors are not. It's really rather a good thing to say because this business is nothing but sales.

Later in the interview, the agent commented further on the importance of sales techniques in the private employment business:

R: You take your best applicants and you work them, that's the way to make money. If you go to somebody's house and you're trying to sell them a vacuum cleaner, back to that, you're talking to this person and they are saying, "Yes, yes, yes . . . ." If you get no objections then you might as well get up and walk out because he is not going to buy, you know. If you get an objection like, "I can't afford it" or "Why?" then, fine, the salesman is in like Flynn because he's got something to fight back with. And it's the same sort of thing with the employment agency business, and I think probably that the majority of employment agency owners don't really realize the amount of sales this is involved in. Everything, I think, always goes back to sales. I'm on that kick.

I: Did you say the owners realize the importance of salesmanship?

R: They (the owners) may realize it, but they don't, I think, impart that information to their counselors . . . . It is sales and some agencies say so and some don't, you know. They prefer to put a more glowing terminology around it.

Several agency owners told a female college graduate with a sociology background who wanted to work as a counselor that they preferred someone with a background in sales. One particular instance is as follows:

Well—out trotted the boss! He was tall, blond, wearing a tab-collared, blue and white pinned striped shirt, a black and white pin striped suit with a matching vest and a college ring. I have seen him before in many used car lots. He led me over to a corner desk and asked me why I wanted to go into this business. I told him I enjoyed working with people and it was a challenge. He then asked me why I did not go into teaching, and I knew he was not going to hire me. He then explained that I needed some real selling experience—"like having closed a big deal." Like having sold taxes. "I need counselors, yes . . . but this is slow time . . . no one is hiring now with all of the kids out of school . . . I'd be crazy to hire you now. You see I have to pay you to draw, which I don't have to pay men. If you turn out to be a flop then I'm stuck." I did little talking and his advice was to get more selling experience.

Another agency told the same young woman that sociology and employment work do not mix:

This agency was run by middle-aged woman. This woman did not idealize the job. She, like the first man I talked to, had a very business-like approach to the job. She said I was not bashful which is a good trait for a counselor, and asked me to call her back in two weeks, when her assistant manager would take over.

This lady was worried about my being a Sociology major, because one had worked for her at one time and tried to save everyone who came in. She said one cannot work that way, because you must be selective with the applicants, because the agency had a good reputation with the employers, and she did not want to ruin it.

Agency owners fully appreciate the skills that are useful to success in the private employment agency business and, consequently, seek to recruit aggressive young men and women with a sales orientation. A typical newspaper ad for soliciting new counselors goes like this: "We are looking for aggressive, young men to start as trainees to become employment counselors. This is selling at a high level with large commissions." Or, department managers may select them from among job applicants who seem to have the requisite salesmanship qualities. Little else seems required.

The initial screening of new counselors by the employment agency management tells much about the job. Here is the experience of one counselor who responded to the agency's advertisement:

I called the agency and asked to speak with the technical-department manager. I told him I was interested in becoming a counselor and asked him when I could come in for an interview. I noticed that on the phone his voice was loud, clear, and quick. He arranged to meet with me later that day.

At the agency, he told me to sit down next to his desk. He studied my card with a look of concern. He asked me why I wanted to become a counselor. As he stared at me intensely and looked over my clothes, I had the feeling he was trying to make me feel ill at ease. Then he would stare at my card again and tap his fingers loudly on the desk; soon, his foot was also tapping as fast and as loud as his fingers.

The technical-department manager then asked me about my experience as a salesman. He wanted to know how much I was interested in selling. Then he handed me a manual to read, which explained in detail how the agency operates with regard to commissions, bonuses, and promotions. Afterwards, I was given a personality test. It sought to measure my disposition toward selling and making money. He studied my test paper for a few minutes. Apparently satisfied that my intentions were clearly to make money, he told me to come to work the next day.

The three prime criteria for a good counselor, therefore, would seem to be: an ability to sell his own personality; a great concern with money; and a neat appearance.

One type that the agency definitely did not want was the "humanitarian," to whom service might be as important as money.

The backgrounds of agency managers and counselors are usually not related to employment work and serve to highlight the diffuse nature of their collective occupational experience. Unlike other occupations seeking pro-fessional status and have not quite made it, such as the semiprofessions of nursing and social work, there traditionally has been no specific background required to become a private employment agent. Kellor's study in 1904 reveals the diversity of backgrounds of early employment agents:

> Investigation shows that a large percentage of intelligence offices are run by persons without business ability or training. It requires no capital and in many states no certificate of character. It is frequently a venture to cover other failure or to supplement inadequate incomes or replenish small losses. Or it is a side occupation, among women combining with washing, sewing, janitress work, or other unskilled labor; among men with keeping a saloon or small shop which the waiting employees can patronize, or running a steamship or railway agency where they can buy tickets.[15]

Today, almost anyone could become a private employment agent and succeed at it. For example, presented below are the backgrounds of the various department managers and ten of the most successful agents at the Midwestern agency which I studied as a participant observer:

Managers
Branch manager: 34, two years of college, former lab technician.

Technical manager: 36, three years of college, former assistant chief engineer.

Chemical manager: 31, no college, formerly a bit player in a local theater group.

Administration manager: 30, college graduate, former high-school teacher.

Agents
College graduate, 24, former professional football player.
High-school graduate, 35, former butcher.
Junior-college graduate, 28, former truck driver.
College graduate, 31, former industrial engineer.
Two years of college, 32, former quality-control expert.
Two years of high school, 41, former junk deaker.
High-school graduate, 26, former door-to-door salesman.
High-school graduate, 27, former insurance underwriter.
College graduate, 23, no previous work experience.
Two years of college, 25, former management trainee.

When asked what "it takes" to become a good counselor, one counselor in our study with three years of experience in two different states blandly said:

> In my opinion the most important factor in being a counselor would be the gift of gab, and the ability to shoot the bull with people. If you can't talk to people you certainly can't pull from them what you need to know to find out what to do. So, being able to query people would be the most important aspect of the business.

He then commented on the types of people who are counselors: "The types of people who are counselors run the gambit. I took a fellow who dropped out in his junior year (of high school), and put him to work and trained him, and made him one of the highest money-makers in our business in Dallas." The counselor also related an interesting example of how even "unattractive" persons, who probably would seldom be hired as a "public-greeter" could be successful as an employment counselor:

> There's a girl in our office, ugly as sin—she's got to be the most hideous woman that I have ever laid my eyes on—27, negative blood factor, crossed-eyed—her eyes are crossed to the point of tolerance. You look at her and you really, you just can't look at her. Applicants can't look at her, but she has an excellent personality and an excellent ability to "interpret" people. She can just look at somebody, and tell you a great deal about

them. We've had an applicant in the office, as a sideline to Jan's abilities, who looked drunk. We were quite sure she was. She had just been laid off, and we presumed that she had been out "celebrating" all afternoon. Jan took one look at her, and decided that was impossible. Her hair was too neat, her clothes were to well arranged for anybody that had been out drinking for any length of time. She didn't look like she had been working up a sweat or anything, and she decided that she could only be an epileptic.

Thus, an essential qualification for the role of employment "counselor" is the ability to "size up" people, which is characteristic of any good salesman.

The employment agent, in his dealing with applicants, relies upon his ability to sell and not upon utilizing a technical body of knowledge. The lack of technical knowledge sometimes impedes the agent's ability to communicate with an applicant. When the job is highly technical, agent comprehension is decreased, while his apprehension is often increased. One agent, described an illustrative incident that revolved around his failure to understand the technical jargon of a professional applicant:

R: I had an engineer, and of course engineers are a sort of a different breed of cat anyway, they're a pretty . . . pretty interesting group of people because of the diversity in personalities that you run into. They're either usually very, very technical, or they are just flat nuts, funny, witty, outgoing people. But anyway he was one of the more technical type people and his vocabulary consisted of nothing but monosyllable words, and he was talking entirely over my head. I had no idea of what he was talking about, and I made some remark about "Well look, I'm sorry I can't even talk to you, you're using vocabulary that I've never in my entire life heard of. I'm sorry I was educated in the field of literature and psychology, and this sort of thing and I don't know the first god damn thing about what you are talking about, you know. So if you can't come down to my level you're going to have to get out of here." And he got up and left.

In further conversation with this agent, he goes on to explain the agent's lack of technical knowledge:

I: That brings up another complaint that they (applicants) have. Someone with technical training would say, "The counselor doesn't know enough about the jobs to know whether or not I'm qualified for it. As a result he 'winds up' sending me out for jobs that I'm not qualified for and the employer doesn't want to see me and I don't want to see the employer . . . the counselor doesn't know enough about the field.''

R: That's a very good point. Most counselors know nothing at all about the jobs that they are talking about. I would say that 75 percent of the employment counselors in this country, I think, the people that I've met around—I've met some people in New York and New Jersey, and they don't know a damn thing about what they're talking about.

I: You mean the content of the job?

R: Yeah, what the job is. If you say you want a computer programmer who uses the Fortran language, nobody knows what it is. And if it is Fortran II it is entirely different than Fortran IV, you know. There are scientific languages. But there isn't a counselor living that knows this unless he's worked them. You just don't, what the hell would you want to learn that for, you know. It's just like the fact that nobody knows that dogs don't have cones in their eyes and don't see color because of it—very few people know that, but it is a fact. But it is just like a lot of other things, no human being can be that retrospect, if he is that retrospect and that capable of knowing that many different things about that many different jobs then he is going to be in a different kind of company to begin with. He's damn sure not going to be working for an employment agency peddling people.

The agent went on to say that he instructed new employees either to not let the applicant know their of ignorance or to confess from the very beginning that they were laymen who would need the applicant to explain his technical qualifications and desires in terms that they could understand:

R: They (good counselors) will not let the applicant know they don't know about their job, or they will flat tell them so. And I have always trained the people that I've worked with to do one or the other. Either ask leading questions without giving the applicant an opportunity to know how deeply ingrained your ignorance is, or say "Well Joe, I'm sorry I don't understand what you're talking about. If you could be a little bit more specific it will help me in talking with these people. Give me key words." And Joe is usually more than happy to help you out. Because he is proud of what he knows and because he knows that without knowing it you are not going to be able to help him out and so forth. But what I think you are talking about is the fault of, it's the situation where you have an improperly trained counselor and most employment agencies—if anything the state could do, they should set up a training program. They don't have to run it, but something that has guidelines.

The profit motive is not the only key factor in explaining why employment agents find sales techniques useful. The inherent sales nature of the job seems to make agents cynical about applicants, as suggested by one male couselor with three years experience:

I think all employment agency counselors tend to "bastardize" the applicants a little bit. There are means and ways of handling them. You get a little cynical when you interview 200 or 300 people over a couple of months—you get to a point where you just cannot reach into these people and make any sense out of what they say. I'm not a psychiatrist either, but you know you get awfully impatient with people. Having hired quite a few trainees and people to work in employment agencies, I find that we have situations sometimes where, where you're training these people you just . . .I don't know, become quite a bit, I don't know, cynical maybe.

The agent then went on to vividly describe a recent situation in which he was led to "bastardize" an obstinate applicant with the help of a test:

Well I had a situation yesterday, an applicant walked in looking for a job. Interviewed him, found he was qualified rather nicely for $600 a month, cost accounts position that I have . . .Well anyway, this particular applicant was just hostile as hell, I mean I asked him where he had been—we ask this information for purposes as counselors. As far as the applicant is concerned, we ask him where he has been and what other companies he's talked to for the purpose of determining whether or not he's "pending," and likely to be considered for hiring from other companies, and also so that we, as counselors, can turn around and call these companies and get their job orders for the same things that he is pending for, and send other people out—it is a matter of course, it's a means of source material. But, at any rate, he was not going to say. And, he said he was really, really, bitter about it, the whole business (of looking for work and using an agency). To get applicants out of our hair we test them. In other words, if it's somebody (difficult to deal with) rather than say, "Have a seat in the waiting room, let me call the employer," I say, "Well, all right, Joe, It's time that you took a test for me. I'd like to just get a general idea of how you come out on our Wunderlick test," which is really a crappy, guided thing. It's a tool. It's a lever to keep them busy for 10 minutes, while we either regain our senses, if it's a difficult applicant, or put them in the proper position—perspective as far as the jobs are concerned, and see about companies for them, you know. Now, many times I will give somebody a test if he is nervous and high-strung, and he just wants to sit still to keep him occupied while I call up and set up appointments for him. I could care less how the test turns out, he'll do for a given type of job because of his background. At any rate, he was really quite bad about the business of giving me information—it was like pulling teeth from turnips to get information.

In spite of the above applicant's unwillingness to tell the agent all that was asked of him, he scored exceptionally high on the test. His test performance was seized by the agent as a device to "jar the senses" of the applicant in order to get him to respond to him. The agent called the applicant back to his desk and said to him:

All right, your test score is exceptional to the point of arousing my curiosity about this. And, I just don't mean to be a horse's ass about this or anything, but why did you come in here and act so goddamn hostile about these things. You've done many things that make me feel like you're not worth sending to anybody.

Challenging the applicant was deemed necessary in order to make him cooperate in a situation where "you are sitting across the desk from a total stranger, somebody that you have never seen before in your life." A direct assault upon the applicant produced more open and cooperative response:

I said (to the applicant), "I don't mean to be rude or anything, or overly personal, but I would like to know just exactly why you are so damned defensive about what is going on here. You are coming here for me to do something for you and you're fixing to pay me a very much over-rated fee for what? The services, for what I'm fixing to do for you, and so forth. So, I would just like to know why you're so damn defensive about it." And, he answered. He replied, and he said that he was very sorry, that he was just nervous as hell. He had never been to an agency before.

This agent-applicant encounter, told from the agent's point of view, suggests that routine sales obstacles (in this case an obstinate applicant) require a workable solution ("jar his senses"). Overcoming sales obstacles is the essence of the private employment agent's job. It involves a process of making the applicant and, if possible, the employer dependent upon him. The more dependent the buyer, the easier it is for the agent to sell him. (The degree of dependency of different types of applicants will be discussed in the next chapter.)

The sales-technique methods used by private employment agents to obtain fees are perhaps functionally equivalent to methods used by some of the established professions. Success as a defense lawyer, for example, is heavily dependent upon the practitioner's ability to convince the client that he is doing something for his money, as Abraham S. Blumberg explains:

The defense lawyer in many ways plays the confidence man. The client is cast as the mark. The lawyer convinces him that pleading quilty will lead to a lesser charge or a lesser sentence, and the eager client agrees, forgetting that in pleading quilty, he is forfeiting his right to a trial by jury and getting a presentence before a judge.

The lawyer's problem is different. He is not concerned with guilt or innocence, but rather with giving the client something for his money. Usually a plumber can show that he has performed a service by pointing to the unstopped drain or the no longer leaky faucet as proof that he merits his fee. A physician who has not performed surgery, advised a low-starch diet, or otherwise engaged in some readily discernable procedure may be deemed by the patient to have done nothing for him. Thus, doctors may order a sugar pill in paying for nothing.

The practice of law has a special problem in this regard. Much legal work is intangible.[16]

Convincing clients that they are being properly taken care of may be an occupational necessity when the client pays the fee. In order to insure prompt payment, the professionally recognized practitioner often attempts to manipulate the client. Blumberg's analysis of lawyer behavior provides a vivid example of this aspect of the professional-client relationship:

Defense lawyers teach even the most obtuse clients that there is a firm connection between paying up and the zealous application of professional expertise, secret knowledge, and organizational connections. Lawyers, therefore, seek to keep their clients at the precise emotional pitch necessary to encourage prompt fee payment. Consequently, the client treats his lawyer with hostility, mistrust, dependence, and sychophancy in precarious mixture. By keeping his client's anxieties aroused and establishing a relationship between the fee and ultimate extrication, the lawyer assures a minimum of haggling over the fee and its eventual payment.

As a consequence, all law practices in some degree involve a manipulation of the client and a stage management of the lawyer-client relationship so that there will be at least an *appearance* of help and service.[17]

There is a parallel between lawyer-client relations and agent-applicant relations. However, it does not provide a firmer basis for relegating agents into the same professional status as lawyers. It merely discloses that clients are vulnerable.

Other aspects of what agents actually do can be gleaned by looking at some of the interaction between agents and their managers. At the agency I worked in, and this is apparently typical of many agencies, both agents and managers tend to be young; the median age for both, in my agency, was 31.

They are young; in part, because the field itself is relatively young. Then too, managers prefer younger counselors, whom they can train more easily. It also seems to be true that most counselors with some experience eventually leave the field.

Still, some of the counselors had considerable experience in employment work, and managers had usually been highly successful counselors before promotion. Although all were supposed to be expert at placing other people, few had had any valuable background experience or training other than counseling. Personality and salesmanship counted most.

The department manager usually hired his own counselors and was expected to be a "driver" with them. He constantly asserted his authority, freely bawling out anyone, even the best counselors, he thought might be loafing. He accepted only one explanation when a counselor "lost a placement"—the applicant had not been properly conditioned.

What does this do to the counselor's self-image? Peter M. Blau has described three basic situaitons that produce feelings of inequality and alienation in employees.[18] Managers inflict all three on counselors. They constantly ride them and aggressively check their work, and in a personal way; they assert their authority through immediate punishments (in my agency, usually a public bawling-out) and immediate rewards; and their exercise of power seemed arbitrary and sometimes almost whimsical.

Still, I found that counselors did, nevertheless, often strongly identify with their departments and the agency. Perhaps they saw reason, even consideration, behind the method: managers told them that they constantly scrutinized their work because they wanted the counselors to make more money; and the punishments and rewards might indicate how important the counselors' work was. And counselors did get quick recognition: when one made a placement, he immediately walked to the center of the office, banged a large brass gong to inform everyone and took a prize from a table loaded with $2 gimmicks.

Moreover, the manager was a "model" to his counselors. As a formerly successful counselor, he could give them expert advice and criticism. They turned to him for guidance. More important, he lent them moral support. When they became depressed by abuse from applicants and employers, he encouraged them and taught them how to accept disappointment. This support can be very important to a counselor because much of his job is deeply frustrating. When he calls an employer about a possible placement, he is in a position of servitude. Employers occasionally become angry about being bothered and may chew him out or hang up on him. The applicants, too, can be very difficult.

Just as the counselor tries to shape the self-conception of the applicant, so the manager shapes the self-conception of his counselors. But he can afford to be more genuinely sincere and understanding.

As might be expected, the turnover of counselors was very great. My agency's manager said this was because "many men cannot take it." By "it" he meant the pressures from employers and applicants; apparently he never entertained the idea that the heavy pressures from him and his department heads might have some effect.

Conditioning of counselors also includes regulating their personal attitudes and behavior at work and even off-duty. The rulebook forbade discussion of agency business in any public places, open fraternization with other counselors in the office neighborhood and fraternization with stenographers anywhere. Counselors were often shifted around, at least partly to discourage friendships, however, some friendships did form.

Under the guidance of their managers, counselors develop a moralizing rationale for the conditioning they give applicants. They are doing it for their own good. Both applicants and employers must be forced to wake up and face reality. "They cannot have what they really want because it does not exist. They have to be like the rest of us." Some counselors believe they are a great help to everyone including society, because they "put people to work." With such responsibilities, they cannot be very much concerned with what individuals want: "They don't know what they want."

Counselors maintain that experience teaches them that applicants and employers pay closer attention to and are more easily led by someone who never asks or suggests but tells them exactly what is good for them. Gradually, then, the counselor's orientation and self-image develop along the line of aggressive salesmanship. And those who adjust best and do not drop out were inclined that way to begin with. One of the more vociferous managers told me that he had had a mean temper before he entered the business—and now his temper was making money for him.

The general characteristics of the private employment agent's drive for professional status can be illustrated in yet another way: by an examination of the recent private employment agency association activity in California. It demonstrates the nature of the realtionship between agency and state.

State Regulation of Agencies—A Shift in Emphasis

In view of the hazardous historical relationship between state and employment agent, can we expect to find a major state allowing agents to regulate themselves? This is exactly what California has done. On September 5, 1967, Governor Ronald Reagan signed into law a bill passed by the legislature entitled, "Chapter 21 of the Business and Professional Code" or A.B. 466. Prior to A.B. 466, private employment agencies operated under the jurisdiction of the California State Department of Labor, as is the situation in most states. Now, agents are under the Department of Professional and Vocations Standards. The assumption underlying the shift in status is that criteria of professional standards have been established by and for agents. Our analysis, however, suggests this assumption is in error.

The California Employment Agency Association was, of course, the interest group that lobbied through this legal status change. There was no organized resistance to A.B. 466, not because agencies in California are highly ethical. While under the jurisdiction of the State Department of Labor, complaints against the abusive activities of private employment agents were regular and numerous. Recognizing this, the California Employment Agency Association (CEAA) created an "Ethics Board" to establish norms for agent behavior and provide sanctions for any individuals who deviate from the set norms. Applying the sanctions is proving difficult, according to one CEAA officer we interviewed.

The shift in legal status has not been welcomed by all agents. In general, the agents with whom we talked believe that the new law would give them a "freer hand" in their work. Several veteran agents felt that the shift in emphasis was a very serious mistake on the part of the state government. A typical criticism indicated that the new law permits the more unscrupulous agents to take advantage of the "freer hand" situation.

The critical veteran agents in our sample were deeply concerned about the image of their occupation. They called themselves professionals and were highly thought of by both their applicants and client-employers (we talked with some of their former applicants and current client-employers). According to the veteran agents, the unprofessional, unscrupulous agents have so damaged the public image of the occupation that it is a source of constant embarrassment for them. The new law was viewed as a setback for true professionalization.

A solo woman agent with 11 years experience who calls herself a "professional searcher," was quite upset with the new law. Her criticism focused on the need to enforce a professional code of ethics:

> Let me tell you, I think that this was very wrong because there are very few people that are operating in the personnel field that are truly professional, and will follow the professional code of ethics. . . .And consequently, you have these people who have no understanding of the code of ethics at all and, yet now, they are looked upon as professional and they have no guidelines, no one over them. Now they have wanted this for many years and they have it. . . .The true professional didn't want it.
>
> Now the individual that doesn't know the difference can be (exploited) because they put on these vast advertising campaigns and there is no one to monitor the advertising. . . .It was required (under the State Department of Labor) if you ran an advertisement in a newspaper, you had to have that position. And not only that, but it had to be nondiscriminatory. Today there is no one to monitor to see if those positions are really available.

When asked if other "abuses" have become especially noticeable since agencies have been placed under the Department of Professional and Vocational Standards, the agent suggested that a "traditional" abuse (fee-splitting) is not being curbed:

When a person stays on the job 90 days, that is considered permanent. Well what employment agencies will do, they'll have a set-up with the company—this happens right here in this area—whereby the day the 90 days are up the individual will be let go. And they have collected their full fee. . . . Now this happens more often than it doesn't happen. Now this was one of the things that when they were under the Industrial Relations that they would get right on to this and clean it up! They would suspend licenses over it. But today this no longer exists. This is one of the things that I've called about not being professional, because the practice is wide open. And there are other practices. I won't name the companies, but I have flat refused their business because the personnel department, the directors or even some of the individuals have wanted a kick-back. . . . But there is no regulation over that now. See there is no one that looks after this and I think this is very bad.

The removal of the state as overseer of employment agency standards has had the effect, according to the same agent, of dissolving all professionally meaningful standards of performance. This has paved the way for salesmen-agents to employ more dubious sales techniques:

I think that an agency should have had to come up to a certain standard and have been proven before they were accepted by the state as a professional. But, this is not so and they put everybody on the same level. In fact, it has discouraged me about the business, you see there are no professional standards at all. . . . Now a company falls just as much prey as the candidates, the applicants, because the company comes into an area and they don't know who is good and who isn't, and who is ethical and who is not ethical, and they get involved with these agencies in the same way and it takes them a couple of years before they find out. Because normally the agencies who do these things have excellent salesmen, and they tell the companies that they are the one and only, and as I say it takes a couple of years for them to realize that they are not scrupulous. Well, I myself, I'm tired of fighting the battles, and I'm not going to fight them any longer.

Another agent, a college graduate who had worked in Texas for three years as an agent and in California for two, also believes that the new law is a serious mistake:

R: I don't mean to be cynical, but it is just irrelevant to me one way or the other. But, I think in California they are going about it all wrong. I don't like at all the idea of each salary in a given salary arrangement being based on a different level. I think that if the state government in California has any responsibilities, you know, to the people of California they ought to do something about it.

I : Well, what they did was to take the employment agencies out of the jurisdiction of the Department of Labor, and placed them in the Department of Professional and Vocational Standards, and let the private employment agencies control themselves.

R: Yeah, which is very bad.

I : Why?

R: In my opinion—because these people (employment agents) are getting away with murder.

I : Could you give an example?

R: I do know that there are just a certain, there's certain types of things that it's wrong to do, and one of them is to try to suck some poor fool into paying his entire first month's salary, you know, for something like this (finding him a job). It's just wrong. It's against every grain of common sense in my body.

Other employment agents, however, were strongly in favor of the new law. Yet, their reasons for supporting the new law were, at times, contradictory! Some felt the old California laws were overly restrictive, and the new law would relax these restrictions to a more tolerable level. Others felt the old laws were too lax, and that the new law would enable the agencies themselves to censure "the few bad agencies that were still around."

One of the agents who felt the "old laws" were too restrictive was a San Jose agency owner who said:

California is the most restrictive of all states. If you can do business and be successful in California you can make it anywhere. I suspect that there are so many restrictions because of early abuses by agencies. The legislature over-reacted. If an applicant didn't pay his fee, we had to go all the way through the Labor Commissioner's office and then through the courts. This has just recently been changed and now we can go straight to the courts just like any other business.

It is not accurate to label the older California laws as "the most restrictive of all states." Numerous states restrict the behavior of private employment agents in two important ways: limiting the amount of the fee charged and preventing an agency from garnishing an applicant's salary or attaching his property if he does not pay the fee. California law did not restrict the agents in these areas.[19]

An examination of the old California laws shows that they were not exceedingly restrictive. The major requirements for establishing a private employment agency were: (1) the agency owner should be a resident of California for a least one year (2) a $1,000 bond should be posted and (3) two witnesses testify to the character of the individual. Although a fee schedule had to be filed with the Labor Commission, there was no restriction on the fee charged. The regulations governing daily business were likewise not severe. For example, the employment agent was required to keep records of his transactions subject to inspection by the Labor Commissioner. Controversies between the applicant and the employment agency were referred to the labor commissioner for adjustment (the decisions were in favor of the agencies 95 percent of the time). An applicant who paid a cash fee but did not receive employment was entitled to a refund. An agency was also forbidden from dividing fees with an employer.[20]

Some agents argue that self-regulation is preferable to a loose system of laws enforced by the Department of Labor. Their main point is that "unethical" agencies can be better policed and, if necessary, more easily eliminated. If this were the case, one would expect to find signs of a "get tough" policy in the new law to insure better service to applicants, or, at least, an emergence of more stringent qualifications required of the agents. An examination of the new law reveals, however, that the major change in qualifications is to make it more difficult for anyone to start an agency. The new requirement states that the individual operating the agency must have two years of "related" experience. The new law also requires that owners, partners and "officers" of the agency must pass a written test concerning retention of the Labor's Administration Code and a list of ethics. There is no test of the agent's familiarity with techniques of vocational counseling or with the job market. The individual agent has only one day or two of instruction before beginning to work with applicants.

In effect, the new law prevents someone from opening an agency without first serving a two-year apprenticeship as an agent. This is to the advantage of agency owners. For a long time, owners lost many of their best agents soon after they learned the tricks of the trade, made connections with local employers and had enough capital to open their own agencies. Thus, the purpose of the legal change in status was not to eliminate abuses, but to limit agency competition.

The push for power led the private employment agents to undertake pseudoprofessionalization, employing psychological and political strategies. The nature of the work performed by the private employment agent requires exceptional salesmanship in order to succeed. The rules of the human marketplace probably govern the extent of ethical and unethical behavior tolerated. This is suggested by data presented in this chapter, as well as by data presented in chapters 1 and 3. Although the claim by the private employment agents that they can police themselves is somewhat less than what is possible. It is difficult, if not impossible, for any occupational group to control its members[21] ethical behavior, especially in this country. This is more intensively the case when it comes to an occupational group that has undergone pseudoprofessionalization.

NOTES

1. Harold L. Wilensky, "Professionalization of Everyone?", *The American Journal of Sociology* 70 (1964): 40.

2. The word "profession" is adopted by an inconsistent and heterogeneous collection of workers. This collection includes not only medical doctors and attorneys such as heart surgeon Dr. Christian Barnard and Chief Justice Warren E. Burger, but also athletes and entertainers such as Joe Namath of the New York Jets and Raquel Welch of Hollywood. Goode has noted, "spokesmen for almost every recognized white-collar job have asserted that they are professional." Yet, clearly, even workers other than those who routinely wear white-collars declare themselves professionals. See, William J. Goode, "The Librarian: From Occupation to Profession," *The Library Quarterly* 31 (1961): 307

3. Since there is no more precise specification of the elements for identifying a profession, whereby occupations might be ranked along a continuum, we can but reiterate the two core characteristics commonly attributed to an ideal-type of profession. The two main criteria identifying a profession are: (a) a technical base and (b) adherence to a service ideal.

The process by which an occupational group takes on the core characteristics of a profession is described as professionalization. Hughes considers this process central to the study of professions: "in my own studies I passed from the false question, 'Is this occupational a profession?' to the more fundamental one, 'What are circumstances in which people in an occupation attempt to turn it into a profession, and themselves into professional people?'"

What occupational groups seek professional status? Usually the more specialized workers, especially salaried employees, are more actively engaged in obtaining professional status. Their professional aspirations tend to influence the status-seeking occupational groups to emulate the visible, established professionals. For example, they begin to call themselves professionals, adopt a code of ethics and form an occupational association.

Such activities, however, seldom incorporate the distinguishing features of a profession.

In American society, the majority of the occupations striving for professional status are failing. See, for example, Peter M. Blau and W. Richard Scott, *Formal Organizations* (San Francisco: Chandler, 1962); Nelson N. Foote, "The Professionalization of Labor in Detroit," *The American Journal of Sociology* 53 (1953): 371-80; William J. Goode, "Community within a Community: The Professions," *The American Sociological Review* 20 (1957): 194-200; Goode, "The Librarian";

Everett C. Hughes, *Men and Their Work* (Glencoe, Ill.: Free Press, 1958); Marvin B. Sussman, "Occupational Sociology and Rehabilitation," in Marvin B. Sussman, ed., *Sociology and Rehabilitation* (Washington, D.C.: American Sociological Association, 1966), pp. 179-221; Howard M. Vollmer and Donald L. Mills, eds., *Professionalization* (Englewood Cliffs, N.J.: Prentice-Hall, 1966); and Wilensky, "Professionalization?"

An operational test for "technical" is when preference in hiring is given to those who proved competence to an agency external to the hiring firm or consumer (e.g., a university or technical school) and that all the necessary skills cannot be learned on the job. A.L. Stinchcombe, "Bureaucratic and Craft Administration of Production: A Comparative Study," *Administrative Science Quarterly* 4 (1959): 168-87.

A service orientation is a professional norm meaning that personal and commercial interests are subordinate to the client's interests when the two are in conflict. This does not mean the same as "client oriented," which sometimes occurs among solo practitioners (Wilensky, "Professionalization?").

4. "Certification Programs Opens New Year," *Placement Age: The Voice of the Private Placement Industry*, January 1968, p. 3 (italics ours).

5. Ibid.

6. Wilensky, "Professionalization?"

7. Howard S. Becker and James Corper, "The Elements of Identification with an Occupation," *The American Sociological Review* 21 (1956): 341-48.

8. Malcom Margolin, "Help Wanted: Honest, Intelligent People to Run Employment Agencies," *Fact*, November-December 1966, pp. 42-43.

9. "Certification Program."

10. Theodore T. Cowgill, "The Employment Agencies of Chicago," unpublished M.A. thesis (University of Chicago, 1928), p. 161 (italics ours).

11. Ibid, pp. 161-63 (italics ours).

12. *By-Laws of the National Employment Association*, Article II, Section 1-2.

13. John C. Holmes, NEA Director of Government Affairs, *Placement Age: The Voice of the Private Employment Industry*, March 1968, pp. 5-8.

14. Margolin, p. 46.

15. Keller, *Out of Work*, p. 207.

16. Abraham S. Blumberg, "Lawyers with Conviction," *Transaction* 4 (July-August 1967): 18-19.

17. Ibid., p. 19 (italics his).

18. Peter M. Blau, *Bureaucracy in Modern Society* (New York: Random House, 1956).

19. Ibid.

20. In 31 states, the placement fees charged by employment agencies are limited by law. Most states allow an agency to charge between 25 percent and 50 percent of the first month's salary. One of the exception states, Montana, will not allow a fee of over $3.00 to be charged, whereas Kansas thinks this is too much—its maximum fee is $2.00. In California the typical agent fee is 90 percent of the first month's salary. For high-paying ($15,000) jobs, 10 percent to 15 percent of the first year's salary is a common fee.

21. Ibid.

5

THE APPLICANT MEETS
THE AGENT

The Nature of the Relationship: Power Dependence

All professional-client, salesman-customer relations involve mutual dependency; each party is more or less dependent upon the other to satisfy a specific need.[1] In the case of the applicant-private employment agent relationship, the basis of dependency for the applicant upon the agent is getting an acceptable job. In turn, the agent depends upon the applicant getting a job through him in order to collect a fee. The applicant and the agent, in this sense, are mutually dependent. Mutual dependency is the most critical factor determining the nature of the interaction between applicant and agent.

The private employment agency, of course, realizes the importance of making the applicant feel dependent upon the agent, which is why a sales orientation is instilled into the agents. In a power-dependent relationship, the person who is more dependent has less power. The problem for the private employment agent, then, is in obtaining sufficient power over the applicant in order to make him accept a job as soon as possible. The organizational solution to this problem is to treat the applicant as a commodity who has more or less market value. The agency operates in a manner that is structured to manipulate the applicant so he can be handled more easily and more easily sold.

For an illustration, let us look at the typical social situation encountered by an applicant at the agency where I studied as a participant observer.

As the applicant enters the glass doors of the agency office, he meets a female receptionist. She asks him, "Have you ever been here before?" If he has not, she hands him a five-by-eight-inch background-information card.

Hastily, she tells him to take a seat in the area to which she points, to fill out the card and to return it to her as soon as he is finished.

Within 60 seconds after the applicant returns his card to the receptionist, one of the department managers, whom the receptionist summoned, rushes to her desk and takes the card. The manager reads the applicant's name aloud. As he approaches his caller, the manager thrusts his hand foward as an invitation to shake. The manager shakes his hand once, briefly but firmly, gives his name, then says, "Follow me" and makes a sharp turn.

The manager walks hurriedly and the applicant is usually racing to catch up. He stops at one of the agent's desks and introduces the applicant to the agent with whom he will be working.

The agent repeats the firm, brief handshake and tells him to sit down in the chair next to his desk. The seat on the visitor's chair is four inches lower than the seat on the agent's chair. This tends to make the agent psychologically "above" his visitor. Like the patient on the couch interacting with his psychoanalyst or the defendant with the judge, the applicant has to lift his head in order to speak with his agent.

The applicant, in short, enters into a setting that provides specific instructions about what he is to do. Once he has complied he has, in effect, agreed to the agency's right to determine his behavior and to make arrangements for and about him. Contractual rights and obligations have been indicated and he has, in effect, accepted them. As Erving Goffman has pointed out, "to move one's body in response to a slight request, let alone to a command, is partly to grant the legitimacy of the other's line of action."[2]

Next, the interview. Individual agents vary in method, but the goal is always the same: to instill in the applicant a sense of dependency in order to control him. The degree of dependency is measured by the extent of compliance. In my agency, the process even had a name: "conditioning." The agent seeks (1) to establish his authority and (2) manipulate, or at least profoundly influence, the applicant's image of himself. The agent must accomplish both of these goals; if he does not, he cannot properly control the applicant.

The general prestige and aura of the agency—its location, furnishings, busy and alert agents—all help elicit favorable first impressions from the job-seeker. Then—sometimes subtly, sometimes harshly—the agent quickly lets the job-seeker know that he is in the presence of an expert and the only way he can get a good job is to cooperate fully and, in effect, do what he is told.

Techniques for obtaining the applicant's faith and obedience vary. One successful agent had been an industrial engineer for nine years before coming to the agency, and continually invoked his experience: "I know, because I was an industrial engineer myself." Another successful agent invoked his years of successful experience in employment work; his techniques had got so many placements for so many people over so many years that how could their efficacy be doubted?

The age of the agent is another factor in controlling applicants, especially older, professionally trained ones. Many of these applicants, in fact, seem to feel the need for a kind of Freudian father figure; they are uncomfortable with counselors much younger than they are.

In several cases, for example, job-seekers called the agency in response to newspaper ads. Over the telephone, they seemed eager to find out what was available. The agent, age 22, made appointments with them to come to the agency.

Soon after meeting with their agent, who was fairly successful in conditioning applicants, the applicants' attitude changed from one of ready cooperation to reservation—a reverse conditioning. In each case, the job-seekers were more than 20 years older than the agent. The applicants probably felt that the younger man was incapable of advising them on an important decision. In these cases, applicant control was impossible. (Sometimes the manager would preceive this and keep older applicants away from young counselors.)

Probably the most important factor that influences conditioning is brought to the agency by the applicant himself: his self-image, his belief in what he is and what he is worth. Most of the applicants at my agency were professional and technical workers with a lot of formal training. They therefore tended to regard themselves highly and to consider their skills valuable. They would not take just any position. They strongly resisted such ideas as a possible cut in pay or moving to another city. So the agent's first job was to psychologically cut these applicants down to size.

The counselor begins by determining how highly the applicant regards himself by (1) asking him to list and rate his skills (even though the agent already has his background-information card) and (2) testing his reaction to hypothetical job offers. The applicant usually exaggerates his skills— probably because of his desire to impress the agent and because he wants to obtain a job that offers the rewards usually given to highly qualified employees. Once the agent is sure of this exaggeration, he sets to work.

First, he tells the applicant about other men in his field who are more qualified in education and experience but are making less money. Even if the applicant already seems to have a low enough opinion of himself this putting-down may be done anyway, to make certain that he retains no secret thoughts about his elevated worth. Second, the applicant is told that, at present, his field is overcrowded. Good jobs are scarce because too many good men with the same skills are unemployed. In a buyer's market, sellers cannot be choosy.

If the applicant does not accept the agent's view of him, the agent has two other courses. He may trade applicants with another agent who might have better luck or he can "show" the applicant by sending him out to be interviewed for a couple of jobs he is definitely underqualified for. Both courses are sometimes necessary for proper "conditioning."

The "Universal Approach"

Ideally, the agent should vary his techniques for each applicant; but, because he has a natural desire to keep using what has worked in the past and because it is easier to make applicants adapt to him than vice versa, many agents use the same techniques—modified only as to degree—for everyone. This is called the "universal approach."

One very successful agent specialized in placing highly trained structural engineers and designers. Yet he would systematically tear down each new applicant, ripping apart his self-image piece by piece. Applicants often became angry, voices rose and politeness disappeared. But after the applicant was sufficiently frustrated and depressed, the agent would indicate that there might still be hope—and start to put the image back together again into a more acceptable, controllable form. In effect he said: "You aren't worth much to industry, but I may be able to do something for you anyway." For him this approach worked, and he wouldn't change it. He said that he couldn't afford to "lose a placement" (have an applicant refuse a job offer) because of inadequate conditioning.

Friendship between agent and applicant is, of course, taboo. "Friendship breeds compassion," and compassion has no home in the private employment agency. An agent who is a friend could cater to an applicant's wishes and might even reverse the relationship, becoming the buyer instead of the seller.

My department manager told several stories to demonstrate the dangers of friendship. For instance, one agent did not obtain the applicant's signature on the contract because he was a friend. (The signature is the guarantee that he will pay the fee if the position he accepts calls for it.) The applicant appealed to their friendship as sufficient guarantee. The young man was sent to an interview for a job, and the terms of the agreement with the employer were that the "applicant pays fee." He was offered the job and accepted. Informed of this by the employer, the agent called his friend to congratulate him. And when the agent asked when he would come in to pay his fee, his friend, the applicant, told him to "jump in the lake."

Of course, the agent may, as a matter of technique or control, want to appear sincere or friendly. The selling techniques are often informal and seemingly friendly—applicant and agent call each other by first names. The agent wants to lead the applicant the way he wants him to go while letting the applicant think he is getting what he wants. But the agent is usually dissembling.

Applicants: A Sample

In order to obtain more useful contemporary information about applicant-agent interaction, we spent nine months part-time gathering interview information. In our interviews we were primarily interested in exploring the nature of the experience of dealing with a private employment agency for different types of people, the consequences of different kinds of experiences for the user's self-esteem and career pattern, satisfaction with the agency's service and further insights into the nature of the private employment agent's relationship with applicants.

Most of the information presented below was gathered through intensive interviews with 63 former applicants of private employment agencies (a sample interview can be found in the appendix). However, the principal investigator has spent many hours engaged in conversation with applicants and agents during the past eight years. Thus, impressions gathered informally have guided and supplemented more systematic data-gathering.

The overwhelming majority (92 percent) of the applicants were enrolled in a master's of business administration program at either the University of Santa Clara or San Jose State College. Brief questionnaires were filled out by the sample in nine classes. Those who indicated they had used private employment agencies were telephoned and asked if they would consent to an interview.

Typically, the sample was composed of young men; 78 percent were between the ages of 25 and 35 (the median age was 30, ranging from 21 to 51 years of age). Occupationally, they mostly were in the lower ranks of industrial management (21 percent), engineering (20 percent), sales (7 percent), computer programming (6 percent) and accounting (6 percent).

Most of the applicants were in or about to enter lower management positions, anticipating successful management careers. All but five had already graduated from college. Sixty-one percent had used agencies more than once and 67 percent had used agencies within the last three years. The occupational stratum we are dealing with is, therefore, the rapidly growing one of college-trained organizational men.

Each interview took approximately one and a half hours. The former applicants were asked 40 open-ended questions. Their verbal responses were tape-recorded and later transcribed into typed manuscripts.

There is a wide range of private employment agencies. We have tried to limit our scope for practical purposes. The interviewers focused primarily on agencies specializing in "professional" placement or "executive" and "management" recruitment. It should be noted that the differences in individual biographies of both agents and applicants cause a qualitatively different interaction between agent and applicant, although agencies try to maintain a particular style. For example, a person accustomed to a subordinate occupational role may be more easily conditioned by an employment agent than a person accustomed to a supervisory position. Our occupational strata are fairly broad. Even within a very limited stratum, personality differences may affect the interaction between agent and applicant. A loud dominant applicant may tend to create a different experience than one who is quiet and submissive, since the applicant helps to shape the interaction process. Even agencies handling the same limited occupational stratum differ in how they treat their applicants. In short, many variables other than dependency influence the nature of the experience. With a large enough sample, time, and financial resources many of these variables can be controlled for. (It is hoped that someday this venture is undertaken.) Within the limitations of this project we were able only to concentrate on obtaining what we feel is a minimally representative sample of the different types of applicants, based upon their degree of dependency at the time they entered into a relationship with the agent. The findings presented should not be considered conclusive, but suggestive.

Applicant Typology

We found that applicants can be meaningfully distinguished on the basis of their dependency upon the private employment agent.[3] Although dependency is a continuous variable that could theoretically take on an infinite number of values, in practice agency-users could be classified into six discrete types who could be ordered along a dependency continuum. It would appear that virtually anyone using a private employment agency would fall into one of these categories. The categories are:

1. Recruited—those actively recruited by an agent
2. Ad-Curious—those who contact an agency in response to reading or hearing about an attractive position available through the agency
3. Shopper—those casually engaged in looking around for a job, stop at agency to see what they have to offer
4. Efficient—those who know specifically what they want, and use an agency to save time and trouble
5. Frustrated—those who turn to an agency after having exhausted other available means of getting a job

6. Desperate—those who need to find employment, even if temporary, immediately.

These six types can be placed along a dependency continuum, from low to high, as shown here:

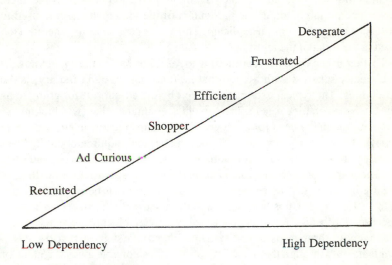

Low Dependency   High Dependency

The recruited applicant initially has the least dependent relationship with the agent. As he enters into the relationship he, in effect, demonstrates very low need for a job. The experience of one recruited applicant is a typical example:

I: Why did you choose to go to the first agency?

R: Because he (the agent) called me on the phone.

I: How did the agency receive your name?

R: He said he received it through the school. I was going to San José State at the time.

I: What was your reaction to the phone call?

R: At first, I didn't want to get involved, because I thought the guy was some kind of a "con" artist. But, when I thought about it, I decided I couldn't lose anything. So, I may as well try it.

Usually, the recruited applicant is already employed. The agent attempts to secure him as an applicant. In many cases, the agent already has a specific position in which he hopes to interest the recruit. "Executive searchers" are the types of agents who normally depend upon recruiting employed applicants. Other types depend primarily upon applicants getting in touch with them. The immediate task for the agent in dealing with recruited applicants is to make them "curious" about better job possibilities. Executive recruiters realize they are dealing with an independent applicant who will not bow to high-pressure sales techniques. A typical sales technique used by agents in their attempts to influence an independent applicant is to point out that he has nothing to lose by learning what is available in the job market. If the agent has a specific job in mind, the particulars of the job create the lure used to influence him to become an applicant. Thus, the agent seeks to generate a job need in the mind of the recruited.

Distinguished from the recruited, who, as far as he lets the agent know, is sufficiently satisfied with his job that he does not make an inquiry, is the ad-curious. The typical explanation given by the ad-curious for going to an agency is seen in the case of a 25-year-old accountant: "I . . .was looking for a job, although my need for a job wasn't pressing. I just wanted some extra money. I saw its (agency) ad in the newspaper and inquired about it. I was mostly curious." The ad-curious applicant has more reason to depend upon the agent than does the recruit. The fact that the ad-curious is willing to inquire indicates that he recognizes the possibility that he might do better than in his present position. The ad-curious usually contacts an agency because of a specific position he learned was available through that agency. The agency, through its advertisement, intends to suggest that the job is available only through them and, of course, does not give away the name of the employer in the ad. The alternatives available for obtaining that specific position appear limited to the specific agency that paid for the ad. This limitation of alternatives may serve to make the ad-curious slightly more dependent upon the agent than the recruited.

The ad-curious is slightly more dependent initially because of a greater need. Actually, the "need" in the usual ad-curious—based on the feeling that he might be doing better—is a potential one that has to be developed. If the ad-curious inquires about the ad over the phone, the agent makes every effort to get him into the office by explaining the necessity for coming in. Once the ad-curious comes in he may decide that the job is not for him. The agent, depending on his technique, usually tries to explain either why the applicant does not qualify for the job or why it is necessary for an agency to place such ads in order to "educate" respondents to the reality of the job market (i.e., "glorious jobs are scarce"). The ad-curious is often disappointed during the initial interview because of the usually misleading ad. As such, he requires a great deal of conditioning by the agent; the "mark" has to be "cooled." The disappointing nature of the initial conversation between the ad-curious and the agent is often difficult to erase.

The shopper has a greater need than does either the ad-curious or the recruited, since at the time he contacts an agency he is already actively engaged in looking for a job. As one shopper said, "I just wanted to see if there was anything around.'' No expenditure of energy was necessary on the part of the agent to attract the shopper. The job need was great enough to prompt him into action. The shopper believes he has several alternatives for finding a job, which is why he contacts the agency in the spirit of shopping around. He perceives more alternatives than does the ad-curious, and the need of the shopper is more immediate. The greater need tends to make the shopper more dependent upon the agency. The agent seeks to limit the alternatives of the shopper. He explains how more efficient it would be if he would simply work exclusively with his agency. If the shopper does work exclusively with one agency, and thus close off alternatives, he becomes more dependent upon that agency. The agent's aim is to make a shopper into an efficient applicant.

The efficient applicant resembles the shopper, in terms of need. Although he is not very pressed, his need is great enough to provoke him to turn to an agency as a matter of convenience. One 30-year-old engineer explained, ''It was the easy way; instead of me doglegging the pavement, they (the agency) provided the service.'' The efficient applicant consciously limits his alternatives. He is aware of alternative means of finding an acceptable job, but the cost of checking them out on his own is, in his view, not worth it. He is usually in a position with limited opportunity for shopping around, and he considers loss of time and money when he decides to use an agency. Usually, this type of applicant has not only a reasonably favorable image of what an agency can do, but also a fairly accurate idea of what he is worth on the job market. Consequently, he approaches an agency with a specific type of position and working conditions in mind, usually directly related to his previous experience or training. While he is more dependent upon the agency than the other three types discussed so far, he has a matter-of-fact attitude toward the agent. It is usually useless for the agent to attempt to condition the efficient applicant into accepting a position that deviates too greatly from what he already had in mind when he contacted the agency. Typically, this type of applicant has marketable skills and can be placed by the agency.

The efficient applicant is normally a cooperative applicant, if the agent will agree to look only for the kind of job he will accept. This applicant generally does not hesitate to use more than one agency in order to get better service. The agency often realizes this and attempts to explain in rational terms to the applicant why it is really more efficient to work with one agency at a time.

The frustrated applicant has been looking around for work for some time when he finally comes to an agency. One frustrated applicant, for example, explained that he went to an agency, ''since none of the other methods worked.'' His attitude often suggests frustration, and the initial interview normally uncovers it. The frustrated feels he has exhausted almost all of the alternative means of finding work. He has tried on his own before going to an agency because typically he has an atittude of ''self-sufficiency.'' It is the lack of reinforcement for this self-image which often accounts for his frustration. With a frustrated applicant, the agent has a pliable person.

The desperate applicant has the highest need of all six types. Although his alternatives may, in reality, not be as limited as the frustrated, he does not have the time to look into them. The desperate needs employment immediately, usually due to the pressure of paying bills. One former agency-user explains why he was desperate at the time he went to an agency, ''At this time I had to make a quick decision. I came to the Bay Area to go to school, and I was looking for some kind of work that I needed quickly. My wife had just had a baby and I had been forced to leave school a few months earlier, so I wasn't trying to be too choosey.'' The desperate, like the frustrated, is easily identified by the agent. In many cases, he will tell the agent he needs a job as soon as possible and is often willing to accept a job that might be considered unaccepptable if he were not so desperate. This applicant has the potential of being the easiest satisfied. Because of this high dependency upon the agent, he follows the agent's advice readily.

Self-Esteem

Assuming that one's self-image is dependent upon interaction with others, especially those who fulfill ''self-relevant'' needs, it may be expected that in our study the applicant most dependent upon the agent would most likely experience most affectation of self than applicants less dependent. However, this was not the case. We found that the most dependent applicant, the desperate, is generally not more affected in terms of self-esteem than other applicants. It seems that the desperate applicant blames his present state of affairs on factors mostly outside of his control. Thus, he approaches an agency with a definition of his situation, which suggests there is little need for self-defining other than recognizing a temporary hiatus. Nevertheless, the recognition of an immediate need for a job is in itself intrinsically distressing for most people. One desperate applicant, a 30-year-old manufacturing engineer, commented on the general affect of looking for work, as he sees it: ''It's the entire business of being without a job. I think the total affect of looking for work is depressing for most people.''

The greatest blow to self-esteem is felt by frustrated applicants. It is characteristic of the frustrated applicant to harbor a self-image of self-reliance, which partially accounts for his personal attempts to find a job, before turning to an agency. It is usually this aspect of the self that suffers the most damage among frustrated applicants. A process of redefining has already started when the frustrated job-seeker decides to become a frustrated applicant. The desperate job-seeker who becomes a desperate applicant, on the other hand, does not need to undergo a process of redefining self since he believes not only that he has other alternatives, including self-reliance, but also that his situation is due to transitional circumstances.

The frustrated applicant's self-esteem is quite damaged from fruitless job-searching before he goes to the agency. Once inside the agency, the agent often tries to enhance the frustration in order to let the applicant know that his frustration is both recognizable and perhaps justified. This is done in order to seize control over the applicant quickly, since it is often necessary to try to ''counsel'' the frustrated applicant into accepting another kind of job in a more accessible line of work. A 30-year-old security investigator explains how this happened to him:

> They (private employment agents) would all say that they had tried to place security people before and that it was practically impossible to do, because it was such a limited field. It was very frustrating when the minute you tell the man (agent) what you are (occupation), he in response tells you, before getting any details or even asking if you want to get out of the field, that you're going to have the same difficult time as the people like you that he's tried to place before.

Later in our interview with this applicant, he notes that a similar instance with another agent really angered him: ''I was even insulted by one counselor, which caused me to leave the agency. And, that bothered me considerably.''

A description of the fairly typical manner in which frustrated applicants are vigorously conditioned by the agent is illustrated in the words of another 30-year-old applicant, who is a sales manager:

> He'll (the agent) tell you what a louse you are, and how you have nothing to sell, and that you couldn't possible get the salary you're asking for; that you've got no experience. Then, he'll tell you how he's going to do all these great things for you. . . . Then, he'll say that he'll let you know in about two or three days, which he doesn't do.

Applicants who use private employment agencies for efficiency purposes are a rather diverse group in terms of their responses and experiences. In general, an efficient applicant who has a realistic conception of his worth in the market is able to avoid the more important implications for self-defining often associated with using an agency. However, an efficient applicant, even one with good job prospects, can easily feel uncomfortable about depending upon a stranger for something as vital as a job. For example, a 31-year-old general supervisor said that going to an agency ''lowered my integrity of myself; it lowered my confidence to a certain degree.''

A discouraging response from the agent is not uncommon among efficient applicants. Discouragement is a normal sales technique of private employment agents, and it is reflected in the experience of a 24-year-old loan officer:

> I : Did going to the agency affect your self-esteem?
> R: Yes, some (agencies) were quite discouraging. They tried to put me into a job that they thought was probably the only type that I could get and that had a poor salary.

Some of the unanticipated consequences for self-esteem arising from using a private employment agency seem to be reflected in the collective experiences of the efficient applicants. Not only discouragement and sometimes distasteful treatment at the hands of the agent may await the applicant, but also a label may be applied by business executives to agency-users. One man, a 33-year-old manager explained that he once lost out on a good job with a large insurance company because the executive conducting the final interview told him that if he did not have enough drive to find a job on his own, then he was not the kind of man they want. This remark hurt his pride more than losing the job offer did.

Another efficient applicant found that his self-esteem was affected by his interaction with the personnel workers in the companies which interviewed him for a job. In many cases, however, it can be expected that the personnel workers resent private employment agencies because they threaten their prestige and existence. Nevertheless, personnel workers sometimes make it uncomfortable for agency applicants, as seen in the case of a 25-year-old product engineer:

> I did notice in some of the interviews the personnel people for the company put me on the hot coals for using an agency, which is something I didn't expect would happen, but it did happen. I think they think that it shows a lack of inititative on the applicant's part.

The experience of an efficient applicant may serve to raise his self-esteem when he does not have a high enough estimate of his worth. A 31-year-old manufacturing supervisor presents an example of this:

> I: Did it (using an agency) affect your self-esteem?
> R: Yeah, I thought it did because I was a . . . like I said, at that time I was hesitant to look for a job because I thought I might have a difficulty or a difficult time getting the money I wanted, and the job I wanted. But actually, I got a job I consider a good job within a week. And, I got real

good response from the agency and from the people I talked to. So it influenced my self-esteem in that I looked good on the market as far as that goes.

In general, the shopper applicants were the most able to transcend the implication for self-defining in their experience with the agency. Thus, it is usual to find a shopper with little or no recollection of his self-esteem being confronted, even when asked in a variety of ways. What perturbed the shopper the most about using an agency was depending upon someone else to find him a job. In this sense, the shopper is similar to the frustrated. One important difference between the two types is that the shopper has not attempted to exhaust his alternatives before going to an agency, which suggests that self-reliance may be more important to the frustrated.

One shopper, a 28-year-old insurance underwriter, explains how using an agency affected his self-esteem:

> I: Did going to an agency affect your self-esteem?
> R: Yes, somewhat. You look at it as someone else doing your work for you.

Another shopper, a 30-year-old sales service specialist was annoyed by the feeling that he had to rely on the agency:

> They (the agency) made me feel as though they were my salvation for finding a job and that annoyed me because I was the one that could and would be selling myself to a position and they were only middlemen for their customers, so to speak.

Later in the interview this applicant made the following remark on self-esteem:

> I: Did going to an agency have any affect upon your self-esteem?
> R: At the time, yes. I felt that I was coming as a beggar, more or less. I felt that there I was: "Here I am, give me a job because I need one badly and I can't find one myself."

A shopper in doubt of his worth to industry may find some positive reinforcement from an agency. If a shopper is especially attractive, an agent will naturally attempt to recruit him as an applicant. Thus, this type of shopper would receive the same special treatment given a recruited applicant. Two shoppers in our sample had this experience. One, a 33-year-old manager, said happily that his experience with the agency, "confirmed my opinion of where my best potential was, not only for success but also for satisfying my self interest.'' The other shopper, a 31-year-old management trainee, maintained, ''If anything it (going to an agency) enhanced it (self-esteem) in that, as I said before, I came away feeling favorably impressed.''

For the ad-curious, the main alteration in image concerned their image of the agencies and the agents. Other than slightly tarnished hopes of a better job, the ad-curious indicate little affect upon their self-esteem. The specific comments of one ad-curious, a 37-year-old engineer, is typical of almost all the ad-curious in our sample:

> I: Did going to an agency affect your self-esteem?
> R: No. I was not unemployed at the time so my feelings weren't that much aroused. I was surprised because I thought that if I were a counselor I could have done a better job than the counselor actually did. I couldn't understand why they didn't review the resume to a greater degree, and what type of job he was looking for; rather than primarily recommending jobs because they had openings at the time.

The most positive affect upon self-esteem was experienced by the recruited applicant. Typically, his idea of self-worth is not merely reinforced but enhanced. A 26-year-old nuclear engineer responded this way to our questions on self-esteem:

> R: Yes, it did. It gave me a feeling that I should ask for more money than I would have.
> I: Did you receive this (information) from the interviews (for a job) or from the employment agent?
> R: From the agent.
> I: How did this come about? Was it because of salaries they suggested to you or just the way they treated you?
> R: It was more or less the way they treated me. I told them what I was making, and at least they gave me the impression that they thought they could get a lot higher paying job.

From our interview material, we may infer that a private employment agency differentially affects the self-esteem of different applicants. As an applicant comes to depend upon the agent to find him a job, almost any action or work from the agent can be construed as either a positive or negative impression of the applicant's worth. The degree to which an agency affects the applicant's opinion of his self-worth is not solely related to the urgency of the applicant's need for employment. This is seen in the case of the desperate, whose need is most urgent. But, because he feels he has not used all his alternatives, he is not as greatly affected as the frustrated, who has, in effect, no alternatives. The only type of applicant who consistently has his self-esteem flattered is the recruit.

Counseling

Most private employment agents call themselves "counselors," not only for creating a more professional image but also to signify their alleged function of advising applicants of the best kind of work available for their particular skills. However, a private agent is not a vocational counselor. According to the agency-users we interviewed, the agent is a "matchmaker," matching available applicants with available employers. This clear-cut function is simply noted by one desperate applicant, a 29-year-old operations officer for a bank, when describing his experience:

> I must have spent all of three and one-half minutes with the interviewer (agent). Then, I was out applying for the job, and as I say, I had the job by noon that day. . . . That was probably a mistake on my part, because I hadn't anticipated that it would be that easy to get a job, and it was the first thing that came along. If I had it to do over again, I think I would probably have been more selective. But, like I said, I needed the work badly, and I didn't have too much time to weigh and choose.

The desperate applicant expects neither a perfect job through the agent nor a lot of personal counseling. He wants action. While career counseling may be useful to him, it is generally not vital since he intends to improve his job status through training anyway.

A frustrated applicant generally does not want counseling. He is typically in a specific line of work. He is not primarily concerned with the salary level but merely with finding a job in his particular line. It is humiliating enough that he has to use an agency to help him find work. As a result, the frustrated seeks neither consolation nor advice from the agent. The typical attitude of the frustrated toward finding a job through an agency is seen in the comments of a 33-year-old quality control expert: "I probably would have taken almost any other job of similar calibre at the time because I needed money."

The frustrated, like the desperate applicant, is vulnerable to the agent's powers of persuasion, although there is less need to persuade the desperate. Usually, the frustrated is the applicant most sensitive to "misleading" sales techniques of the agent. For example, a 30-year-old sales manager reports:

> I found many (agents) who did try to pressure me, many (agents) who were unfair, many who made glorious promises, which they had no intention of keeping, many who attempted to mislead me about what the job market was.

The matter-of-fact attitude of the efficient applicant leads him to expect that the agent would pay attention primarily to finding him the specific type of position he desires. The efficient applicant is already decided upon his career and type of position and, thus, does not desire vocational counseling. In fact, a common complaint of the efficient applicants is that they were the recipients of "counseling" when they neither desired nor needed it. When counseling is given to an efficient applicant it is, in the opinion of the applicants, aimed to talk him into accepting a job from the openings available to the agency. One industrial salesman, 28 years old, relates how he was involved in such a situation:

> I: Did the agency try to change your mind as to the type of work you wanted to do?
> R: In some cases, yes. They were obviously anxious to secure me a place, because they would, therefore, get the commission.
> I: What method did they use?
> R: Just persuasion, trying to convince me that in the long run that this would work out to be exactly what I wanted; saying other clients in the past of a similar nature had done the same, and everything had worked out and was fine now.

Since he has a clear idea of the kind of position he would like and is qualified for, the efficient applicant is not easily persuaded to accept a much less desirable job. The agent, on the other hand, can easily misperceive the attitude of the efficient and attempt to treat him like other applicants who come in voluntarily. This apparently happens quite often. When this occurs, the agent usually is unable to gain control over the applicant, and the latter ends up "kissing off" the agent, as seen in the experience of a 29-year-old operations officer:

> I had been in and out of college like a yoyo, because we had had financial problems from the start. As a result, I had an unsteady work record, and I had just dropped out of law school. But, I had graduated from San Jose State with a 3.8 "A" average in economics, and I felt I was worth something to somebody. But, I couldn't convince (the agent) of that. He kept mentioning listings to me, that were so far below anything I was interested in, that I found it very discouraging talking to him; and he finally sent me out on an interview with Dunne and Bradstreet credit checking service. The job turned out to be sitting there and draining people on their bills, all day long, eight hours a day, five days a week, in an office that looked like it had been hit by a large bomb, for very low pay. Secretaries were all over the place, papers all over the place. Not only that, the agency wanted some exorbitant fee. I told (the agent) that I wasn't about to pay a fee of any kind, because I had done that with the first agency and considered that I could do as well for myself. The only advantage to having an agency was to have a reference service available,

and for that I wasn't about to pay the kind of fee that they were asking. I am sure that the fee that they were asking was considerably higher than the fee I paid to the first agency I went to . . . I don't recall the percentage. I believe it was darn near one month's wages. And I told (the agent) that I wasn't going to pay it. I think that cooled him off and me. There again he was a sales person, and to be an effective sales person, you have to control your prospect. I think he knew that he wasn't going to be able to control me, to the extent that he wanted, so he lost interest. I lost interest in him in a hurry. After that first interview with him I kissed it off.

If the agent fails to recognize the precise nature of the attitude and dependency of the shopper, then the consequence is infrequent success at placing him. If a shopper cannot be made more dependent upon the agent through conditioning prior to receiving any job offers, it is usually useless to try to convince or counsel him to accept a job which is not to his liking, especially when it involves a salary lower than what the shopper deems acceptable. A 32-year-old engineer illustrates this point:

I: Did the counselor try to change your mind about the type of job?
R: Yes, as a matter of fact, he did. I had kept the first interview appointment that he made. We had a very nice discussion regarding the products the company made and whatnot, what the work would entail and so forth. Then we got to the point where salary was discussed and they made an offer and I about fell off of the chair because it was so low. I told them that frankly, living being what it was and what I felt engineers were getting in Rochester, that this just didn't seem like something I ought to accept at all. Their immediate response was, "Well, if they're paying that well in the city, then perhaps we ought to consider more, and we really hadn't thought that much about it you know." If it's money, in other words, then let's talk. I couldn't blame them for trying, I guess. But as I recall, it was at that point that I told them that I would require a certain amount of money per month and we parted at that point, and each of us wanted to think about it a little bit more—they about money, and me about other other aspects of the job. I phoned the counselor after that to tell him how the interview went and his immediate response was that I should take the job with the money that they had offered me. However, I didn't believe it. I think I would have rather stayed where I was, really, than have done that. And a day or so later the company called me back and agreed to the rate which I had requested. And that rate which I requested was, I can honestly say, was a fair rate for engineers of a couple year's experience. So I feel that the counselor in that particular instance was rushing things a little bit too much. . . . I regarded the man in the private counseling business as being a man of knowledge in his field, of knowing

something about the rate which I was worthy of. And so when he suggested that I take the job this was a little of a blow, and I guess you could call it an amount of coercion, because it was certainly a weighted opinion and it did make me consider accepting it some more. But actually the rate was low enough that I just couldn't. Had it been closer to the amount which I had requested, however, his suggestion could have been enough to throw the decision the other way.

Another shopper, a 33-year-old accountant, had a similar experience. He felt that it was simply a general problem to be expected of employment agencies: "No contact that I ever had with an agency resulted in my getting a job. They tend to undersell you and send you out on jobs that are less than what you aspire to."

The ad-curious applicant naturally expects a response from the agent on the particular ad in which he was interested. We did not find any ad-curious applicant who experienced a positive response from the agent concerning his chances of obtaining the job advertised. In all the cases we examined in depth (seven), and a number of informal contacts, the agent always tries to "counsel" the ad-curious into considering other job possibilities. The experience of a 23-year-old black ad-curious applicant is typical:

I asked about that particular job (junior accountant), but the interviewer never answered me about that particular job. He tried to line me up. First, he said I didn't have education qualifications. By the ad in the paper I did, but when I got down there I didn't. He asked me if I was interested in being a field representative, which was just a fancy name, but all it was was knocking on people's doors asking them to pay their bills. I felt that I wouldn't do that and it was just the whole atmosphere of the whole interview.

The experience of the recruit was, of course, the most pleasant, regarding counseling. The agent merely offers a "communications service," and lets the potential recruit think about the position himself. The low-pressure selling is vital to success in placing recruits, since they are actually independent of the agent. The agent is more dependent upon him. Consequently, recruits may be bothered by a number of phone calls from different agents, but seldom are they high-pressured.

Satisfaction with Service

After the interviewees described their experience at private employment agencies, we asked them about their opinions of the services rendered by the agency and whether or not they were satisfied with any particular aspect.

None of the applicants were completely satisfied with every aspect of dealing with an agency. Indeed, as will be demonstrated in the next section, there are a variety of areas of applicant criticisms and suggestions for improvements for better agency service, which vary with the nature of the agency experience. Satisfaction with service, by itself, deserves special treatment. This varies directly with the extent of dependency rather than with the nature of the experience. Dependency together with expectations, both stemming from needs and alternatives, influence the applicant to perceive relative satisfaction with the agency service.

The desperates, for example, when asked, "Were you satisfied with the service you received?" indicated a general satisfaction. When he went to the agency, the desperate was willing to accept any reasonable job, perhaps less than what he really thought he deserved, but for only a temporary period. The agency satisfied his need and, consequently, he was relatively satisfied. In the mind of the desperate, a compensation is made for better service (and hence a better job) because he considers the circumstances in which he became an applicant. When asked "Generally, how was the service given by the agency?" one desperate applicant, a 30-year-old engineering manager, reveals the kind of allowances desperates usually make in assessing their satisfaction with the service they received from an agency:

> When I went in (the agency), they slapped an application in my hand that took 45 minutes to fill out before they would even talk to me, and that annoyed the hell out of me. I found that aspect undesirable. But, I understand this is the way they all operate, and then I needed a job.

In marked contrast to the desperates, the frustrated applicants are on the whole dissatisfied with the services received from the agency. Although almost all the frustrated found employment through the agency, which satisfied them at the moment, they felt that the actual service was poor, mainly because the agents had little or no perceived personal interest in their problems. As noted earlier, the frustrated did not desire counseling that attempted to change their mind on the specific type of work. Yet, the frustrated expected that the agent would work harder than he actually did in order to find an opening. For example, a 34-year-old software manager felt that there was actually no real service provided:

> I find that they (agents) don't provide any service for me. What they basically do is keep my resume on file so that they can contact whoever they know in the industry, and place me. But, as far as I'm concerned, they don't do anything specifically to help me.

While the efficient applicants had widely varied responses, most indicated that the service was neither satisfactory nor unsatisfactory. Instead, they chose to evaluate the agency's services in terms such as "mediocre," or "as best as can be expected." There was no efficient applicant who expressed an extreme feeling of either highly favorable or highly unfavorable. The most satisfied efficient applicant in our sample was a 30-year-old computer programmer:

> Well, some of the agencies were very conscientious. They had me going on interviews almost every other day, or two, or three. And, every time I did go, they treated me like a prospective client. I was there to do business with them, either they would get some of my money, or the company would pay them (the fee). So, they treated me accordingly. And, in general, I think they did a real good job.

Another efficient applicant, a 31-year-old manufacturing supervisor, who found the service "acceptable," describes his experience in this manner:

> I went in (the agency) after working hours. It was one of these deals where I was going to night school at Loyola, so I got off work and drove down to see this guy (agent). It was at six o'clock in the evening, or something. And, he waited for me to get there. When I went up to the office, he was the only guy there. So, we sat down and talked for about forty-five minutes. He said fine, and about two days later, he called me up and he had me set up with a couple of interviews. So, it worked out fast, and it wasn't a hectic type of thing, with just him and I in the office.

The agent with whom the manufacturing supervisor dealt made an effort to get what the applicant wanted. Because of this the efficient applicant said, "Oh, yes, there was good service. I can't complain. I didn't like the guy too much, but he did a good job for me."

The opinions of the shoppers were somewhat more variable than those of the efficients. While the majority of the shoppers' responses indicated neither satisfaction nor dissatisfaction, there were some shoppers who expressed a highly favorable or unfavorable feeling about the services of the agency. This is largely due to the unexpected interest shown by the agent, whether or not a job was found for the applicant. One shopper, for example, went to an agency to see what was available for him and received very pleasing service:

> I: In general, how was the service given by the agency?
> R: Very outstanding. They didn't find anything for me at the time, but they were calling me at my home for two and three years after the time that I first went in. They had a tremendous follow-up. That was one thing that really favorably impressed me about that place.

It should be noted that the above applicant, unlike the typical efficient, did not have a specific position in mind when he went to the agency, and therefore could be pleased by a larger number of job possibilities.

Another shopper, who had very low satisfaction with the agency's services states his feeling as based upon the absence of real service:

I: In general, how was the service given by the agency?
R: Poor. Literally, no service. It was a mailing service at best.

This kind of disappointment can be expected to occur among a small percentage of shoppers who go to an agency with an image of their job not warranted by their experience.

None of the ad-curious was satisfied with the services of the agencies they went to. All felt the service was of little value to them. A typical response by the ad-curious is seen in the case of a 31-year-old salary administrator:

I: In general, how was the service given by the agency?
R: I thought it was very poor. I mentioned that I wasn't placed through them, and I question very seriously the possibility of them even having the jobs they list in the paper.

The disappointment felt by the ad-curious is evident in this applicant's answer. Further commenting on the service of the agency, this applicant says later in the interview, "I really doubt if they do much of a service, though possibly they do. I personally felt that I had something to sell when I went to the agency, and they didn't produce in either case."

The recruited applicant is usually satisfied with the services of the agency because he receives a better offer than his present job. For example, one of the recruited applicants expressed his satisfaction with the service in the following way: "The guy (agent) sent me out on a couple of interviews, and I got the impression he was really trying to get me a job."

Criticism of Agency Behavior

While dependency is the most useful explanation for understanding the interaction experience between agent and applicant, dependency alone cannot explain the types of criticisms and suggestions offered by our sample of applicants. Since criticisms formed the basis for suggestions, we will examine them first.

The main criticism of the desperate applicant is that the agent does not seem to be concerned with the "overall" job market; that is, the agent will naturally try to place the applicant in the first available opening the applicant will accept. What is available is what the agent tries to sell. A 30-year-old engineering manager elaborates on this point:

> I really think they (agencies) give you a distorted idea of the kind of work available, because when you walk into an agency, the only thing that is available is what he has listed, and to him that is the entire market. And, he'll try to convince you that's the entire market without taking into account your special background and abilities.

The frustrated applicants agreed for the most part with the criticism of the desperate, which in neither case is surprising when one considers their experience with the agent. The agent sells his "wares" to willing people when he deals with desperates and frustrated. One frustrated, a 30-year-old sales manager, states simply an opinion shared by almost all applicants: "They're (agencies) not generally honest about what the job market is. You have to learn what the job market is for yourself."

With the efficient applicants, another area of criticism emerges. The efficients are divided between those whose major criticism is that the agents are unqualified to make a judgment on their work qualifications and those whose main "beef" is the misinterpretation of the job market, as noted by the desperate and frustrated applicants. One explanation for the first criticism is the disproportionate number of highly technical workers who make up the bulk of efficient applicants (e.g., computer programmers, heat transfer specialists). The thinking of the efficient applicant who complains about lack of proper understanding of his qualifications is seen in the comments of a 25-year-old marketing specialist:

> They gave me some psychological tests, which they didn't have anyone on the staff who comes near interpreting it. It was a short answer thing. It would give a couple words "a funny thing that happened to me was" and there were a hundred and some like this and they wanted to interpret your candid answers. Well, it takes somebody highly qualified in this area in the field of psychology to fully interpret my responses. They were more concerned over that little test, like he'd say, "you didn't react to these spontaneously." I said, "I did." I took my time to put together a proper sentence, but he wasn't satisfied with my answers. And I thought how petty. There was hardly any mention made of the courses or background I had, why I was qualified, I just didn't feel that my real qualifications were appreciated. Many companies (are) like this, I don't think they're geared for college people.

Even though about half of the efficients single out the agent's inattention to special skills, almost all efficients note the agent's misinterpretation of the job market.

The shopper's typical criticism does not deviate from those of the desperate and frustrated. One shopper, a 35-year-old certified public accountant relates the typical shopper view:

His knowledge of the jobs themselves and the people involved was very superficial. I don't think that he ever had real personal contact with the companies and he didn't know the unfavorable aspects of the jobs they had available, or if he did he never passed this type of knowledge on.

Because of the special disappointment of the ad-curious during the initial interview, it is not expected to find the usual criticism taking the form of cynical remarks about the personal orientation of private employment agents in general. To the ad-curious, agents are insincere and not interested in finding the right job. The comments of a 31-year-old salary administrator illustrates this feeling of most ad-curious applicants:

I noticed at (specific agency) that the counselor didn't seem too concerned with his job. I think that was one of the problems. I think that the agencies should get counselors that are serious about getting other people jobs and are interested in their problems.

The recruited tends to compain about the "number of calls" from different agents, trying to interest him in a position. Other than this, they skipped over the idea of criticisms and focused on suggestions for improvement.

Suggestions for Improving Agency Service

All of the applicants have suggestions for improving agency service. The most common suggestion from the desperates is to recruit more qualified agents. This view is expressed by a 29-year-old operations officer:

I think employment agencies could be a lot more effective and justify their existence more if they were not using commissioned sales people as counselors. If they had salaried employees with backgrounds in sociology or some related field so they could understand the forces that they were dealing with and would work on applicants as something else than a potential commission check.

The suggestions of the frustrated were somewhat similar to those of the desperates. Their suggestions focused on creating more agent interest in applicants and better communication between agent and applicant. This is succinctly stated by a 30-year-old security investigator. He suggests, "A little more sincerity on the part of the counselor and individual rapport between the counselor and the recruit.'' A similar suggestion is made in a more complex manner by a 34-year-old software manager:

> I've been satisfied with the kinds of positions that I've been offered, so I can't say that they could do better as far as jobs go. They could probably be a little more honest with some of the younger engineers about what their potential in salary is. I have had some of the younger engineers working with me get discouraged and quit. They are told that they can get X dollar salary increase (from an agency), but they are still naive enough to believe that six months later they will get a 10 percent raise, and I think this is something employment agencies should point out. Sure, they can get you a new job with a 15 percent pay increase, but you may then be a year away from your next salary increase.

The efficient applicants appear to take special note of the conflict of interests between agent and applicant. They recognize the difficulty of working together efficiently, to the satisfaction of the other. A 25-year-old products engineer expresses how efficients analyze the situation of the agent:

> There's a conflict of interests there and, that is, the sooner they get you a job and the easier, the better the return on their investment, namely their time. So, on the other hand, if he doesn't give you some service he can't stay in business, and he's got to get you a job. That's his first thing, and hopefully get you a job that you're somewhat satisfied with so he can get return business.

The most common suggestion of the efficient reflects the typical one of more knowledgeable agents. A 29-year-old assistant manager suggests this as a major improvement:

> I have the feeling that some people who are employment counselors are not qualified to be employment counselors, (they) are not of the same education and background as the people that come to them, and consequently I don't see how they can counsel. How can someone who has only been an employment counselor tell someone in banking like myself what's available and how to go about getting a new position. I think employment counselors should be a little older than they are, many of them are very young. You wonder how much they know, or if everything that they know is written on the index card in front of them sent by the company.

Increased personalization of the agent-applicant relationship is the second most common suggestion of the efficient applicant, as explained by a 32-year-old management systems analyst:

I suppose that they could spend more time getting to know the individual that they're dealing with. It's important that they do this. It is also important that they get to know their clients very well, which in my estimation they don't know very well. A good number of the more prominent agencies have a large clientele that they have gathered because of the reputation of the agency, and it's had a snowballing effect. And many companies are almost as naive as many employers, myself for example on occasion, and will place an employment order with an agency because it is reputed to be a "well-known and good agency," but they haven't any idea of who they're dealing with or vice versa. It becomes kind of an impersonal thing. So I think there needs to be increased personalization between the agency and the clients they represent, and vice versa. The same kind of personalization that exists between a company and its own personnel department.

Perhaps the essence of the suggestions from efficient applicants can be synthesized by the comments of a 24-year-old loan officer:

Professionalize them. They should have counselors who are qualified and who know what's going on, who are sincerely interested in placing a person in a job not only to get their fee, but to have the person in a job that he enjoys, and the employer to have someone who he can really use. A counselor who is truly interested should be a prerequisite. I think there should be possibly laws or legislation controlling the operations of agencies so that they don't become just a lucrative business.

Almost all the shoppers suggest that the agent develop more familiarity with the qualifications required for different jobs. This is a logical suggestion, considering the utility of such knowledge to the shopper. The view of a 28-year-old insurance underwriter expresses this aptly:

Maybe if they had offices large enough to gather information from all over about what is available. That's the main thing—to improve their knowledge of what's out there so that someone looking for a job can see what is needed and what the qualifications are.

A similar suggestion is offered by another shopper, a 31-year-old manufacturing engineer, who includes his own detailed suggestion on how to accomplish the same end:

Since most of the applicants don't know exactly what kind of job that they would like, I think that it would be advantageous to the agency to have a list of general categories and specific job titles with what they do under each, so that the applicant can say, "Oh yea, I think that I'd like to do that.'' Then, the counselor can ask him what his qualifications are, and tell him whether or not he can fulfill those jobs.

The ad-curious applicants are especially concerned with the attention paid by the agent to their special abilities, which to the ad-curious is insufficient. The major suggestion offered by the ad-curious is that the agent should correct this blight and become more involved with the individual applicant. One applicant, a 37-year-old research specialist, makes this type of suggestion:

They should spend more time on the applicants and possibly give them some tests to determine their likes and abilities. And they should try to place them in positions which they want, rather than in jobs that just happen to be listed with the agency at the time.

A 25-year-old junior accountant, ad-curious, indicated a similar thought about what constitutes a necessary improvement:

The whole key to it is the counselors. They have to be intelligent enough and prepared to really get involved with the people who go to them. They should be aware of and concerned about the psychological motives, needs and aims of the people who come to them.

The recruited applicant simply makes the routine criticism that more emphasis should be made on satisfying both employer and employee. What is especially different about the comments of the recruited is the absence of self-involvement in their suggestions. A 27-year-old mechanical engineer makes this suggestion:

I kind of picture the employment agent as a guy who is interested . . .in meshing jobs with qualifications. I know he has to make a buck, so the guy can afford to live, but I kind of feel that there should be more emphasis on trying to arrange a good guy for the employer, and a good job for the employee rather than just trying to bring the two together so that he can make his dollar. But, I can't blame them for their attitude. They're just trying to get you a job.

The suggestions for improvements, which stem from criticisms, of the different applicants can be summarized and interpreted as follows: Although they obtained a needed job, the desperates realize they were put in the first possible opening in order for the agent to earn a quick fee. Consequently, desperates complain about being given a distorted view of the labor market and suggest that agents become more concerned about the personal problems of their applicants. Frustrated applicants note a similar tendency on the part of the agent. They dislike it, and would prefer better communication between agent and applicant. A "friendlier" agent to the frustrated would be an uplift after disappointment in job-searching. Because the efficients usually know exactly what they want when they go to an agency, they quickly detect the lack of technical knowledge of the agent and occasonal attempts to condition the efficient to lower his job slights. The efficients typically complain about the information gap and suggest closer communication between agent and applicant in order to bridge it. The shoppers want to know what is available for them when they go to the agency, only to discover the agent does not know as much as they had hoped. This is their major criticism. Naturally, the shoppers suggest greater familiarity with the job market would improve the services of the agency. With a specific job in mind, the ad-curious finds the agent not particularly interested in placing him in that particular position. As a result, they criticize this generalized agent trait and suggest that agents become less aloof and more involved with the applicant. The recruited applicants were, for the most part, outside of the area of experience of the other applicants. They did not experience the specific shortcomings of the others. Consequently, the recruits are detached toward agency practices and seem to simply suggest that the agent do a better job.

Agency Affect Upon Applicant's Career Pattern

While the desperate applicant is the type most likely to be placed by a private employment agency, the job he acquires through it is likely to be temporary and relatively unimportant in his occupational career. However, it occasionally happens that a desperate applicant is channeled into a certain field by the agent, which ends up as a permanent occupational area. This is especially true for many desperates who are placed soon after graduating from school in a sales position. One desperate in our sample had this happen to him: "It (the agency) got me my first job out of college, and I've been in that same field ever since." Nevertheless, we suspect this is not typical of the desperates in general. It should be noted that the desperate usually pays the agency fee, which indicates that the calibre of job is not highly desirable. In addition, the salaries for such jobs are often relatively low. Thus, the type of job in which a desperate is quickly placed is usually below their long-range expectations.

The frustrated applicants are most likely to both obtain jobs through an agency and pay the fee for what they want. Yet, in our sample they all found that the job they received through the agency had virtually no promotion possibilities. In accepting a job with little chance for promotion, the agency may have had an indirect influence upon the career patterns of the frustrated. However, the fact that the frustrated were unable to find an acceptable job on their own tends to negate such a possibility. It appears that frustrated applicants do not have sufficient proficiencies to obtain the best available jobs within a specific field. Their dealing with an agency reflects rather than changes the direction of their career.

The efficient applicants had fixed careers in mind at the time they went to the agency. Their dealings with the agent did not alter the plans of any efficient applicants in our sample. There is no clear pattern to the fee arrangements for the efficient applicants who found jobs through the agency; half (four) of those who found jobs paid the fee, the other half (four) did not. About twice as many (17) efficient applicants found no job through the agency.

Shoppers seldom find jobs through an agency. Since they had fairly satisfactory jobs already, they would not consider another position unless it was more attractive. The five shoppers who found jobs in our sample did not have to pay the fee; it was paid by the employer. The shoppers who found better jobs through the agency indicated a turn for the better in their careers, but the influence of the agency was indirect in their view; that is, the shopper feels that the job was available for a person of his qualifications, the agent did not open up a new area of opportunity for him.

Since none of the ad-curious in our sample were able to find jobs through an agency, we might conclude that the private employment agency had no affect upon their career patterns except to shatter hopes for a glamorous job.

As for the recruited, it is not difficult to imagine a turn for the better through the services of the agency. We did not find in our study any first-hand knowledge of a recruited applicant who found better opportunity and changed career pattern through a private employment agency, but it does happen.

The nature of the relationship between applicant and private employment agent is largely determined by the particular power-dependent relation established in the course of social interaction. Almost every likely applicant-agent power-dependent relation could be ranked along a dependency continuum such as the one developed here.

The explanatory power of the dependency continuum developed in this chapter was tested with data gathered on a sample of former agency applicants. The continuum proved effective in differentiating in a sociologically meaningful manner six different points along the continuum, ranging from low to high dependency. The six points are identified in applicant typological terms: (1) recruited; (2) ad-curious; (3) shopper; (4) efficient; (5) frustrated; and (6) desperate.

It was then possible to make a typological analysis of some important consequences of interaction between applicant and agent with varying degrees of dependency. The consequences studied were from the point of view of the former agency applicant in the areas of self-esteem, the nature of the counseling experience, satisfaction with agency service, criticism of agency and effect upon applicant's career pattern.

The data suggest that the social situation of mutual dependency is so complex that logical expectations are sometimes amiss, but not by much. For example, it would be logical to expect that around the point of greatest applicant dependency, designated by the term desperate, would cluster the greatest amount of negative disturbance to self-esteem. The data suggested otherwise. The frustrated, rather than the desperate, indicated the most negative effect upon self-esteem.

The least negative effect upon self-esteem was experienced by the recruited, the point of least dependency. In general, the recruited applicant experienced no negative and some positive effect upon his self-esteem. The experience with the agent is usually flattering for the recruited and he is usually satisfied with the agent's services. The recruited is, however, critical about the number of telephone calls from different agents trying to recruit him. For improving the agent's business practices, he suggests that the agent try to satisfy both employer and applicant. It is quite possible for a recruited applicant to obtain a better job through an agent, although none turned up in the sample.

The ad-curious indicates a very slight negative effect upon self-esteem, stemming from dampened hopes of a better job as advertised. Seldom does the ad-curious receive a positive response from the agent regarding his chances of actually securing the glamorous job advertised (none in my sample). Instead, the agent tries to counsel him to consider other jobs. The ad-curious is typically not satisfied with the agent's service. The agent is criticized as being insincere and insensitive to applicant needs. He suggests that agents get more involved with applicants to learn more about special, individual skills. Career plans were largely unaffected.

The shopper is the one type most able to transcend the implications for self-defining. The counseling experience usually revolves around the agent trying to condition the shopper into a more dependent applicant, but the shopper tends not to succumb. Satisfaction with service is the most variable of all types; sometimes a shopper is highly satisfied, sometimes highly unsatisfied. This type typically criticizes the agent for popular reasons—lack of intimate familiarity with the human marketplace. It is suggested that agents learn more about job qualifications. Those shoppers who find jobs usually improve their careers.

Avoidance of damaging implications for self-defining is usual for the efficient. Having already decided upon his career, he is not persuaded otherwise. He desires a matter-of-fact relationship with the agent, but the universalistic approach of many agents leads them to misperceive the efficient. The efficient is unenthusiastic about the services received and tends to be very critical about the agent's limited knowledge of the marketplace and individual qualifications. He suggests agents act more professionally. Career plans are seldom affected by interaction with the agent.

The frustrated applicant suffers the greatest blow to self-esteem. He is the most sensitive to the persuasive counseling powers of the agent. Generally, he is dissatisfied with the service received and is critical of the agent for placing him in the first available opening rather than taking greater care of him. He suggests that agents take a greater interest in the applicant, learn to communicate better. Career pattern is not usually improved, and often it becomes less bright than he had expected.

The self-esteem of the desperate is generally not much more affected by the interaction with the agent than the other applicant types, since he usually blames his desperate state of affairs on factors outside of his control; therefore, his desperate situation is not a true reflection of his self-esteem. He expects and receives little counseling; he wants a job immediately. The service received is usually considered satisfactory, but like the frustrated he criticizes the agent for placing him in the first opening. He suggests that agencies recruit more qualified agents. The desperate's career pattern is typically unaffected because the job taken is seen as temporary. Nevertheless, once a job is taken, even temporarily, it can sometimes become a permanent one.

NOTES

1. Richard M. Emerson explains that the dependence of one party provides the basis for the power of the other:

Social relations commonly entail *ties of mutual dependence between* the parties. A *depends* upon B if he aspires to goals or gratifications whose achievement is facilitated by appropriate actions on B's part. By virtue of mutual dependency, it is more or less imperative to each party that he be able to control or influence the other's conduct. At the same time, these ties of mutual dependence imply that each party is in a position, to some degree to grant or deny, facilitate or hinder, the other's gratification. Thus, it would appear that the power to control or influence the other resides in control over the things he values, which may range all the way from oil resources to ego-support depending upon the relation in question. In short, *power* resides implicitly in the other's dependency. (Italics theirs.)

The components of dependency are need and alternatives. Need refers to the "motivational investment" in consciously and unconsciously sought gratifications. Alternatives refer to the availability of means of satisfying the need outside of the relation. These components are not discrete categories but continuous variables. The need for the other person's services may vary from extremely vital to virtual indifference. The alternatives to meet the need may likewise vary.

These two variables combine to yield a certain amount of "power dependence," to use Emerson's term. In a mathematical example, $X + Y = Z$. As X and Y take on various values, the third variable Z also takes on a range of values. It could happen that different sets of values for X and Y will result in the same value for Z. Likewise, it could happen that different values of need and alternatives will result in the same amount of power dependence. For example, person A may have a very mild need, but he may be unable to find more than one source satisfying this need. In this situation, there is likely to exist a moderate state of dependency upon the source of need fulfillment. Person B, in contrast, may have a very high need but have available a number of alternatives. Persons A and B, with different combinations of needs and alternatives, may be equally dependent upon those controlling the resources to meet their needs. In general, need is a more important determining factor of dependency than alternatives. Alternatives are really "enhancing factors." Without need, alternatives would be meaningless.

The economic terms of supply and demand appear similar to the components of dependency (alternatives and need, respectively), but as Emerson points out, the term dependency is preferable over these economic terms, "because it facilitates broader application, for all we need to do to shift these ideas from one arena of application to another is change the motivational basis of dependency." From Richard M. Emerson, "Power Dependence Relations," *The American Sociological Review* 27 (February 1962):32-33.

2. Erving Goffman, *Asylums* (Chicago: Aldine, 1962).

3. Each transcribed interview was read by five judges. Much to our delight there was a consensus on each applicant based upon the stated reasons for using a private employment agency for the first time. Since the raw number of applicants is relatively small it is not meaningful to present differences in percentage frequencies in order to highlight differential responses. Our concern is with an analysis of different kinds of applicant experiences with private employment agencies. This distribution of the various types of applicants is as follows: desperate, 4; frustrated, 8; efficient, 25; shopper, 15; ad-curious, 8; recruited, 3.

6

PRIVATE EMPLOYMENT AGENTS IN A TECHNOLOGICAL SOCIETY

Private employment agents play a large and ever-increasing role in the economy that apparently is valuable to industry. Today, almost all large firms (those with over 100 employees) and most of the smaller ones pay all or most of an agent's fee for placing a worker. The agent's role is also valuable to job-seekers, who pay the rest of the fee.

The people who own or work in the private agencies tend to regard them not as social utilities but as money-making businesses. They deal with a commodity. They use aggressive salesmanship to process it and to sell it. They face growing and tough competition because they serve a growing market. Their income comes from fees. Fees come from placements. The faster and more certain the placements, the greater and more certain the income. As they see it, proper conditioning of the applicant is the specific means to achieve more and quicker placements.

To perform this conditioning, the counselors themselves are specially selected and conditioned. Hard-driven, manipulative counselors create compliant applicants with altered self-images. And this is the commodity they send to market. From the commodity's point of view, what is the usefulness of the private employment agency?

The Usefulness of the Private Employment Agency

When the sample applicants were asked if they felt that private employment agencies were a useful business, almost all agreed. The desperate applicants uniformly believed that agencies could be useful to some people in a tight situation, or who might have little desire to go through the hectic process of finding a job by oneself. A 30-year-old engineering manager explains this in detail:

> I: Do you see private employment agencies as a useful business?
>
> R: Well, yes. I think so. There are a lot of people who need the help that the employment agency can provide them because it gives them a friendly atmosphere to walk into and arrange interviews with people; whereas, a lot of people are reluctant to approach a business firm directly. They find it easier to go into an agency. There are also technical agencies that I imagine have their place. There are executive agencies that probably provide a service to a larger corporation seeking managerial help that isn't always available on a local basis. And, I understand that they have large national files that arrange interviews from state to state. That's a legitimate function.

While the answers of the desperate reflect the personal situations people sometimes find themselves in, as they did when they went to the agency, the answers of the frustrated reflect a concern with a specific occupational area. The frustrated believes that agencies are useful primarily in certain fields rather than situations. A 30-year-old security investigator is one who feels this way:

> I: Do you see private employment agencies as a useful business?
>
> R: For certain career fields I think they are, especially the accounting field and certain engineering fields. In the offices that I went to, the lowest fields of placement were, surprisingly enough, engineers and personnel-type people.

Another frustrated applicant, a 33-year-old paint salesman, believes that for people like himself an agency serves a useful purpose:

> I think they can be (useful), very definitely. I know that when I was looking for work, I was almost catapulted into using them. Apparently, many manufacturing companies are using them as a screening device.

The efficient applicants also responded in the affirmative, but many felt that the agencies were not as helpful as they could be. In their view, they could be more efficient. A 32-year-old systems analyst explains this position:

> I have not been impressed with the efforts that the agencies that I have dealt with make. I think the majority of them—well, like everybody—are

interested in making a good living. I think that they become preoccupied with this in many cases to the detriment of the potential employee.

Several of the efficients clarified their answers by specifying the types of people whom could best profit from using an agency, as did this 29-year-old assistant manager:

I think they serve a function. I don't think the ones that handle a broad spectrum are extremely useful for higher level jobs. For young people looking for their first or second job in an unfamiliar area can do well by going to a private employment agency, and being led into the right types of interviews. I don't think that they can handle management and technical people as well perhaps, as these people can find jobs for themselves.

Another efficient applicant, a 32-year-old management trainee, explains how employment agencies should be used:

Yes, depending upon how you use them. I think you should use them to test the market, I would never take a job through them again. If I came into contact with a good job through them I would wait awhile, maybe a year or so, and then try to get in on my own. I would never pay them, even if the employer was supposed to pay the fee I think that at some point it would come out of my salary—that 10 percent to be paid would come out of my first raise, let's say.

All of the shoppers believed that private employment agencies were useful. The shoppers are fairly secure in their present positions when they go to an agency. Perhaps this is why, in their responses, they specified dependent people as the ones who could benefit the most from using an agency. For example, a 26-year-old sales service specialist answered: "Yes, I think that they find jobs for people who can't otherwise find them, but I think that it's the easy way out."

Another shopper, a 34-year-old program manager, had a related comment to make: "If it's useful it would be for an individual that is apprehensive about talking to people and personnel departments. This, then would serve as a go-between, or spokesman to get them started."

Even the ad-curious, who were the most dissatisfied with their experience at the agency responded, for the most part, in positive terms to the usefulness of agencies. They believed that an agency is more useful for some types of persons, those more dependent. Most ad-curious agreed that the potential for agencies was greater than their present practices.

The recruited applicant did not feel he needed agencies. As one stated: "abolish them." But, agencies probably serve a useful function for recruited applicants in that they make them realize they are worth something on the labor market and may even serve to keep their salaries high by making competitive offers.

Expected Future Developments

While social predictions are inherently precarious, they constitute an enticing experience. The viability of even the most mundane, seemingly realistic predictions of the past is often lessened by unanticipated influences upon social change. For instance, Ben Franklin once said that nothing is certain but death and taxes. This has become less certain in a society accustomed to heart transplants and legal tax loopholes. The latter is a historical extension of status privileges, whereas the former is a product of advanced technology.

Heart transplants are only one of many recent (albeit, more dramatic) examples of how technology has helped transform our perception of human control over destiny. The worldwide participation in the moon landing through electronic media, and the shared knowledge of it as shared experience, is not without significant consequences. Whether or not this means we are becoming a "global village," in McLuhan's sense, may not be as important as the recognition of a great technological feat—putting men on the moon.[1] Thus, in order to articulate the logical directions of future social change, we must confront and come to terms with technology.

Two contemporary thinkers, Kahn and Weiner, have offered a sophisticated projection of society up to the year 2000, taking into account technological innovations.[2] They predict that all personal services (e.g., laundries, restaurants, motels, etc.) will continue to capture a greater proportion of the gross national product. This growth will be the result of a saturation of the consumer goods market. With the annual median income projected to rise as high as $12,000 by the year 2000, most people will be able to buy the goods they want and still have enough money to purchase luxury services. Higher incomes will permit the development of service industries. In addition, ample employment and a steady economic growth are promised by Kahn and Weiner. This would be a fertile condition for private employment agency development, since in the past agencies tended to flourish in times of affluence.

However, affluence in the future, unlike affluence in the present and past, *may not require ample or full employment*. Machines can free much of the work force from jobs it now holds. If rapid displacement of men from jobs takes place on a large scale, numerous societal adjustments will have to be made, such as vast retraining programs. For the individual living in such a society, a psychological adjustment will have to be made. If Durkheim, Wilensky and Ladinsky are correct, work as a source of identity will become

more important, especially among the upwardly mobile.[3] Displacement
from work, then, may also be a displacement of self-identity. Those affected
in this manner will require a mechanism by which identity can be easily and
quickly switched from one basis to another. This is not to suggest that the
importance of family, ethnicity, religion and community will necessarily
diminish greatly as sources of self-identity. Indeed, it is possible that the
traditional sources of identity will be revived. Another possibility is that
leisure activities may take on greater self-defining meanings on a mass scale.
At any rate, the fit of man and job may be a critical concern for a rapidly
growing number of people. It is this concern that will probably provide
tremendous numbers of employment agency applicants.

Perhaps one consequence of a technological society with an increasing
number of people displaced from their jobs is a massive turn toward private
employment agents to locate positive identity-generating jobs. If benevolent
wisdom prevails among policymakers, then the abundance of a technological society will lessen the biological motivations for looking for a job (i.e.,
everyone could be housed, fed and given spending money). In such a
situation, a job would almost necessarily have to be the ''right'' job before a
person decides to work rather than simply exist with machine-workers.

The question then arises, who will decide who should do what work?
Michael Young would have us believe that extensive testing periodically
would determine who is best qualified to do a specific task.[4] Everyone would
rise and fall according to their performance on merit exams. This mythical
meritocracy described by Young would grant extraordinary power to the
testers, those who create, administer and interpret the exams. Those who
make decisions over others render the recipients more powerless over their
lives. However, there are forces militating against the development of
Young's meritocracy. One important pocket of resistance comes from the
power elites, who for oligarchical and other reasons will not allow their
positions of power to be threatened by a class of testers.

A more likely development is a large-scale growth of employment services offered by employment middleman, in a variety of disguises. An
organized, entrepreneurial response to the growing need for occupational
counseling is already visible. The most well known of these is the firm called
Chusid. This is an ''executive counseling'' agency where executives are
advised of their talents and guided to more suitable jobs, for a large fee.
Recently, such firms have been the object of governmental investigations,
stemming from complaints filed by former applicants. In New York, for
example, a complaint filed in October 1968 revealed an experience apparently shared by other applicants:

An advertising man complains that he paid Chusid $1,975 and in return
received only psychological tests, two practice interview sessions and

clippings of newspaper ads for positions in areas other than the one he was seeking. He says he paid an additional $178 for "motivating letters" and resumes sent to 650 firms.[5]

The Federal Trade Commission issued a complaint the same year to another firm similar to Chusid, National Executive Search, Inc., of Washington. It charged, "the firm misrepresented the nature, type and effectiveness of its services."[6]

These counseling firms differ from the usual private employment agency in their fee policy. A private employment agency usually collects its fee after the applicant is placed in a job, whereas the executive counselors collect fees before any service is rendered and whether or not a job is found. The profits of such firms are considerable. Chusid claimed earnings of $404,000 on revenue of $5.4 million in the fiscal year ending September 30, 1967.[7] Since almost all of the applicants to Chusid and similar organizations are already employed, they appear to go voluntarily to the agencies in response to advertisements, which stress the importance of self-insight as a necessary prerequisite to the proper fit of man and job. Thus, there are apparently unsatisfactory, or doubtful self-images among many, perhaps most, of the Chusid applicants.

Chusid may be a historical forerunner of things to come. The firm itself may be aware of its potential growth. Fifty percent of middle-top management of firms listed in the New York Stock Exchange are supposedly listed with Chusid. Perhaps in the near future private employment agents or counselors will have permanent records of the majority of people seeking employment, if not everyone. What would be some of the logical consequences of this?

First, it would not be difficult for any organization or person with sufficient financial resources to utilize technological means of gathering, storing and classifying detailed biographical and occupational information of millions of workers. It is only logical to expect that private employment agencies and similar organizations with diverse labels are now turning to computerized methods of data handling. This means that every individuation, every mistake a person makes in his social life may be recorded in the agency files. The question now becomes, what uses can be made of this information?

Throughout history, private employment agents in pure and mixed form have functioned as communications intermediaries. An agent informs his applicants about job opportunities, often manipulating the information as a sales technique to influence the applicant to follow his advice. As we have seen, this can be done in various ways, from misleading advertisements to hiring a piper to recruit workers. The adage, "He who pays the piper plays the tune,'' may be a useful beginning point for understanding the likely social consequences of computerized employment agencies.

If employment agents become storehouses of information on the members of the labor force, they may evolve into clearinghouses for employers. They would be agents of the power structure. The power of workers, including high executives, over their careers would be limited by the agent, who, by the nature of his job, feeds information to employers. As more workers become applicants, whether knowingly or not, with information files held by the agent, the agent is in a position to play a significant role in determining applicants' careers. Unless Young is correct it will be employment agents who may utilize testers and not the testers per se who will likely gain extraordinary power in a technological society. The extent of their power will be limited by several factors.

The most important limiting factor is the response by the government. Public employment agencies were established in reaction to public outrage at the flamboyant abuses of private agencies. By creating an alternative to private agencies, the government is making society less dependent upon the private group. Consequently, the government takes away some of the power of the private agency, which is a form of indirect social control. But public agencies deal primarily with unskilled and semiskilled workers and consequently are not taking away any of the growing pains of the private employment agencies.

It seems that in a democracy, or in a society that at least pays lip service to democratic principles, political forces should develop to check the power of any special-interest group. For example, it is almost fashionable for the military-industrial complex to be under heavy criticism by people who supposedly fear special-interest group power. How does the government limit the power of private industry and occupational groups? Can the government compete with the private sector? Setting up state and federal public employment agencies is one way the government limits the power of private employment agencies. Another example comes from the health field, wherein public health services were established by the government to check the power of the medical profession through preventive medicine.[8]

There is a definite power conflict between the government and private industry that reaches an apex in a technological society. The power of private employment agents and other communications intermediaries is likely to be checked by the government through maintaining alternative means of obtaining information. This is seen not only in the case of employment agents but also in other rapidly growing occupations functioning as communications intermediaries, such as travel and dating agencies. The State Department Passport Bureau, for example, is taking on travel agency functions by providing routing information to people. Perhaps in the future the government will enter into the dating agency business. When the government goes into business it is often done in order to create alternatives for fulfilling a social need, thereby checking the power of the private alternative, which is a form of indirect social control. It also means that more services are being defined as essential and provided as an extension of the rights of citizenship.

The social substance of the future is, in essence, a mystery. "In the year 2525, if man is still alive," are the words to a song that was popular in the late 1960s. It suggests a concern for man's plight and a recognition of his absurdity. If there are private employment agents in the year 2525, who will control them? The National Employment Association is developing enough political power to predict that agencies will be almost completely self-regulating in the near future. Will they be able to control themselves? Once agencies become primarily self-regulating, it would take a concerted public effort to regain control over them. Will public agencies eventually share almost equal power with their private counterparts, or will there be primarily one or the other? Will the meaning of the agent's work (placing people in jobs) change in the eyes of society? Will work itself become more or less of a basis of self-identity?

NOTES

1. See Marshall H. McLuhan, *The Medium Is the Message* (New York: Random House, 1967).

2. Herman Kahn and Anthony J. Weiner, *The Year 2000: A Framework for Speculation on the Next Thirty-three Years* (New York: MacMillan, 1967).

3. Durkheim, *Division of Labor*; Wilensky and Ladinsky, "From Religious Community to Occupational Group."

4. Michael Young, *The Rise of the Meritocracy* (London: Thomas Hudson, 1961).

5. *The Wall Street Journal*, October 11, 1968, p. 1.

6. Ibid.

7. Ibid

8. George Rosen, *The Public Health Service* (New York: M.D. Publishers, 1961).

APPENDIX:
Sample Interview

I: Have you ever been to a private employment agency?

R: Yes, in 1952.

I: Where was the agency?

R: Buffalo, New York.

I: How many agencies did you go to?

R: Just one, I can still remember the name, Green Employment Agency.

I: Why did you go to the agency?

R: I couldn't get a job any other way.

I: How did you happen to chose that particular agency?

R: Just through the telephone directory.

I: Were there other agencies listed?

R: Yes, this happened to be an agency on the way into downtown Buffalo, it was easy to get at.

I: Did you find employment through this agency?

R: Yes.

I: What was the job?

R: I was a chemical analyst at General Mills.

I: Were you satisfied with the job?

R: Yes, I stayed there about two years.

I: Why did you leave?

R: I got a better job.

I: Did you ever again find a job through an agency?

R: No, I never found a job, but I've been negotiating through agencies. More recently in the last three years.

I: Where are these agencies?

R: The agency that I'm working with now is a professional agency. I've been interviewed by one of their people here in Santa Clara during some of the fall joint conferences, computer conferences, and they basically carry my resume and when they receive a position that they think may interest me they contact me, just by phone, strictly by phone.

I: Were you in any agencies between this time you were in Buffalo and the agencies that you're using now?

R: No.

I: How many agencies have you been to in this area?

R: The agency that I'm working with right now is Albert Associates; it's not exactly in this area; it's a national firm. It's main office is probably in New York City, but there are regional offices in Albuquerque, New Mexico.

I: You're just using one agency now?

R: I'm actually employed and trying to find another job. I've been contacted by two or three others, there is Cadillac Associates and they don't seem to be quite as good as this Albert.

I: About how many agencies would you say that you've been to?

R: Excluding the first one, four. Two of them, I talked with them, but they never produced anything. Cadillac Associates seems to produce jobs that are more functional, down in the working area. And Albert Associates seems to go in more for management, they're the ones that I work with most often.

I: I'll be asking you a series of questions about employment agencies, you'll have to answer them in sort of a general way and if there are differences between the agencies, point them out. Did the counselors seem generally interested in finding you a job?

R: When they found out that I was in the computer field they were. I have a feeling now with both agencies that they realize that it is easier to place somebody with a computer background. This is how they make their money, so as soon as you say you're in software computers they try to latch onto you.

I: When you first went to these agencies, including this one, did you have an idea of what kind of work you wanted to do and what level salary you wanted to start at?

R: The one in Buffalo, no I didn't have any idea where I wanted to start. I was still going to school for my B.S. degree. So I really didn't have an idea of what the salary range would be. I remember being given an offer which was $70.00 a week and I took it. As I got smarter, however, I realized you could command a little better salary than that. Now with the current agencies, I am familiar with what the salaries are and I can more or less state what I am looking for.

I: In either case did the counselors try to change your mind as to what kind of work you wanted to do or what level salary you wanted to start at?

R: No. I'll hedge that a little, both the agencies that I'm working with now, basically leave the salary negotiations up to you and the person you will work for.

I: You mentioned that at the point you're at now you don't have to contact the agencies because they will contact you?

R: Periodically, every 3 to 6 months, the agencies that I have been in contact with will contact me and ask me if I am still interested in jobs. If I say yes, they say all right we will contact you as soon as we find something along that line.

I: How did you make initial contact with these agencies?

R: While attending a computer conference during the fall. This was back in Las Vegas about three or four years ago.

I: Going back to the agency in Buffalo, what did the agent say then your chances were of finding the kind of work that you wanted?

R: Well, first I wasn't too particular about the kind of work. I wanted the first job that I could get. He knew that I had some college background, so what he was trying to place me in would be some kind of blue-collar job or white-collar job, and I would suspect that he gave me the first thing that came on his desk that he thought I could fit into. I really didn't have a preference and he didn't give me any.

I: What did the agencies that you're in contact with now say that your chances were of finding the kind of job that you want?

R: I have three offers right now that I'm evaluating, possibly I'll take one. The chances are very good, although they don't state it this way.

I: Did anything the counselors said or do, either at the Buffalo agency or the ones you're using now, make you feel uneasy?

R: The ones that I use now, everything is done over the phone. They're really national search agencies. The one back in Buffalo, probably the thing that bothered me the most was that I remember that he made phone calls right when I was sitting there. He'd call somebody up and say "I have this young man here with Blah blah blah this kind of qualification, could you use him?" He had a little black book with the names of people that he called. I was a little nervous when he went through several pages and hadn't found anything. But outside of that I find that the people that are in this kind of business are very friendly. I don't know how they are if you actually sat there or if you are untalented, but I find them very easy to get along with.

I: Did the Buffalo agent find you a job while you were sitting there?

R: No, but he had found me one by the end of the week.

I: Generally, how was the service given by the agencies?

R: I find that they don't provide any service for me. What they basically do is keep my resume on file so that they can contact whoever they know in the industry and place me. But as far as I'm concerned they don't do anything specifically to help me. I always feel that I'm helping them, and conversely they help me keep informed on the field and salaries. Usually I jack up my salary about 15% per year, and they usually seem to be able to find someone who's willing to pay that much, or more.

I: When you made your initial contact with them at this computer conference did you talk with a representative of the company?

R: Yes, I guess you would call him a representative, there was a member of the firm, in fact it was the guy's wife. You fill out a very brief resume all that they are interested in is your current field, your pay scale, what area of interests have you had, or are you in. They are more interested in current information of what you're doing and how long your've been doing it. Then when they find something that they think you'd be interested in they contact you and send you the name of the interested company and have you contact somebody there, and then the company sends you their application form, for more detailed information.

I: Did you sense discrimination for or against you at any of the agencies that you used?

R: I found a kind of reverse type discrimination, they prefer talking with people that they can place more easily. And I guess if I were a ditchdigger they would just say that's not our field. If I were in a professional area that didn't have quite as much demand they might not have been quite as responsive.

I: In what area of the city are the agencies?

R: I have never been to their offices.

I: What about the one in Buffalo?

R: It was in one of the main buildings, the Lafayette Building, which was right on the downtown edge of Buffalo.

I: How many counselors did the agency have?

R: Just one.

I: Did it have a receptionist?

R: There was a desk there for one, but I got in very early and she may not have gotten in yet. The room had several cubby holes formed by partitions which meant there were several counselors or one counselor would use the room to handle several applicants.

I: Who paid the fee at the agency?

R: At the first one when I was inexperienced, I did. After that the company did.

I: How large a percentage of your salary was it?

R: It was one month's salary payable in four installments.

I: What do your friends say about private employment agencies?

R: They all use them.

I: Did your contact with the agencies have any influence on your career?

R: Yes, I won't say it was the agencies, but the one in Buffalo did place me in a position where I was involved in food analysis and this kept me out of the factory line and made me more sensitive to this kind of thing, and helped motivate me to finish my education. The ones now keep me informed on the latest demands in the field, and I plan my career accordingly.

I: Did your contact with the agencies have any influence on your self-esteem?

R: Yes, the ones now offer increases in the range of 25% over my present salary, and it gives you a feeling to be able to turn these people down. I have been satisfied with my position and now and in the last three years the offers I've received have been about equal or worse. So the money compensation at least for me right now is secondary.

I: Would you leave your present job if a counselor had an offer for a better job?

R: I'm working on three offers right now.

I: Do you see employment agencies as a useful business?

R: Yes, I think they're good from two standpoints. Like one offer I have right now is from a Los Angeles firm that is in a lot of trouble in one area. They are looking for a man to pull together a team to bail them out, but they don't want to go out on the open market. First off they would waste a lot of time, secondly they don't want to tell people that they do have problems. Having a professional agency like this allows a company to get discreet help, in specific areas. And the agencies that I have worked with do do some sorting, they won't just hand your resume around the country. I've never used an employment agency that's not Lockheed's policy, but if I were in a position to use one, it would probably save you time.

I: Does going to an agency give you a good idea of the kinds of jobs that are available?

R: Yes, these particular agencies when they contact you spell out the requirements pretty well, and this tells me what kinds of jobs are opening up and in what field.

I: What ways of improving private employment agencies would you suggest?

R: I don't know, I've been satisfied with the kinds of positions that I've been offered, so I can't say that they could do better as far as jobs go. They could probably be a little more honest with some of the younger engineers about what their potential in salary is. I have had some of the younger engineers working with me get discouraged and quit. They are told that they can get an X dollar salary increase but they are still naive enough to believe that 6 months later they will get a 10% raise, and I think this is something employment agencies should point out. Sure they can get you a new job with a pay increase, but you may then be a year away from your next salary increase.

I: How did you find the job that you have now?

R: (laugh) I found that through *Science and Technology Magazine*. In one of these ads, you know, contact so and so.

I: What method do you consider the best for finding a job?

R: Your personal contacts. Even though I have received these offers through private employment agencies, I am well enough known in the computer industry that people in the computer industry know my name and they made recommendations, and I assume that this is one reason that the dollar and cents offer is better than you expect to get just walking off the street.

I: What was the best job your father had while you were a teenager?

R: Floor supervisor at Kinger Company.

I: About how many years do you expect to remain in your present line of work?

R: If you're saying with the company that I'm with, not too much longer; if you're saying within the computer industry, probably for 25 years.

I: Do you have a good chance for promotion where you work now?

R: No, I'm at the department manager level right now and the next step is program manager, I'm probably too young for that, and besides I don't think the company recognizes software, the area that I'm in as an integral part of their operation.

I: What type of work would you try to get into if you could start all over again?

R: I don't think I would change my line of work, but I would change my background, I would want a broader background.

I: What type of employer would you like to work for?

R: If they could afford my salary and the location that I want— California—a small firm of about 40 people.

Selected Bibliography

Published Files and Documents

By-Laws of the National Employment Association.

Commerce Clearing House Publications on Equal Employment Opportunity. Commission Case Decisions on Racial Bias of Employment Agencies (1972).

National Industrial Conference Board. *The Conference Board's New Index of Help-Wanted Advertising.* Technical Paper no. 16 (New York, 1964).

United States Congress. House. Committee on Education and Labor. Public Employment Service. Hearings, 88th Cong., 2d Session., H.J. Res. 607. Washington, D.C.: U.S. Government Printing Office, 1964.

United States Department of Labor. *Manpower Report of the President, March 1973.* Washington, D.C.: U.S. Government Printing Office, 1973.

United States Department of Labor. *State Laws Regulating Private Employment Agencies.* Fact Sheet no. 5. Washington, D.C.: U.S. Government Printing Office, April 1966.

Published Sources

Abbott, Grace. "The Chicago Employment Agency and the Immigrant Worker." *American Journal of Sociology* 14 (November 1908).

Adams, Leonard P. *The Public Employment Service in Transition, 1933-1968: Evolution of a Placement Service into a Manpower Agency.* Ithaca, New York: New York State School of Industrial and Labor Relations, Cornell University, 1969.

Bakke, E. Wright. *A Positive Labor-Market Policy: Policy Premises for the Development, Operation, and Integration of the Employment and Manpower Services.* Columbus, Ohio: Merill Books, 1963.

Bendix, Reinhard. *Nation Building and Citizenship*. New York: Wiley, 1964.

Blau, Peter M., and Schoenherr, Richard A. *The Structure of Organizations*. New York: Basic Books, 1971.

Commons, John R., et al. *A Documentary History of American Industrial Development*. Vol. 9. Cleveland, Ohio: A.H. Clark, 1910.

Conant, Eaton H. "The Evaluation of Private Employment Agencies as Sources of Job Vacancy Data." *The Measurement and Interpretation of Job Vacancies. A Conference of the National Bureau of Economic Research*. New York: National Bureau of Economic Research, 1966.

Durkheim, Emile. *The Division of Labor in Society*. Glencoe, Illinois: Free Press, 1947.

Emerson, Richard M. "Power Dependence Relations." *American Sociological Review* 27 (February 1962): 32-41.

Gannon, Martin J. "Sources of Referral and Employee Turnover." *Journal of Applied Psychology* (June 1971): 226-28.

Gerth, H.H., and Mills, C. Wright, eds. *From Max Weber: Essays in Sociology*. New York: Oxford University Press, 1946.

Glotz, Gustave. *Ancient Greece at Work*. New York: Barnes and Noble, 1965.

Goffman, Erving. *Asylums*. Chicago: Aldine, 1962.

Haber, William, and Kruger, Daniel H. *The Role of the United States Employment Service in a Changing Economy*. Kalamazoo, Michigan: Upjohn Institute, 1964.

Hall, Jerome. *Theft, Law, and Society*. Indianapolis: Bobbs-Merrill, 1935.

Harrison, Shelby M. *Public Employment Offices*. New York: Russell Sage Foundation, 1924.

Helmold. *The Chronicle of the Slavs*. Translated by Frances J. Tschan. New York: Columbia University Press, 1935.

Hughes, Everett C. *Men and Their Work*. Glencoe, Illinois: Free Press, 1958.

Huntington, Emily H. *Doors to Jobs*. Berkeley, California: University of California Press, 1942.

Johnson, Miriam. *Counterpoint: The Changing Employment Service*. Salt Lake City: Olympus, 1973.

Kellor, Frances A. *Out of Work*. New York: Putnam, 1915.

Lester, Richard A. *Manpower Planning in a Free Society*. Princeton, New Jersey: Princeton University Press, 1966.

Levitan, Sar A.; Mangum, Garth L.; and Marshall, Ray. *Human Resources and Labor Markets: Labor and Manpower in the American Economy*. New York: Harper and Row, 1972.

Liebhafsky, E.E., ed. Perspectives on Manpower. Columbia, Missouri: Interdisciplinary Graduate Program in Manpower, Division of Advanced Studies, College of Administration and Public Affairs, University of Missouri-Columbia, 1972.

Marx, Karl. *Das Capital*. Vol. 1. New York: Modern Library, 1906.

National Urban Coalition and the Lawyers' Committee for Civil Rights Under Law. *Falling Down on the Job: The United States Employment Service and the Disadvantaged*. Washington, D.C.: National Urban Coalition, 1971.

Pirenne, Henri. *Economic and Social History of Medieval Europe*. New York: Harcourt, Brace, 1937.

Polanyi, Karl. *The Great Transformation*. New York: Beacon, 1957.

Pound, Roscoe. *The Spirit of the Common Law*. Cambridge, Massachusetts: Jones, 1921.

"Public Employment Service in the Nation's Job Market, 1933-1963." *Employment Security Review* 30 (June 1963).

Reed, Anna Y. *Occupational Placement*. Ithaca, New York: Cornell University Press, 1946.

Rees, Albert, and Shultz, George P. *Workers and Wages in an Urban Labor Market*. Chicago and London: University of Chicago Press, 1970.

Ruttenberg, Stanley H., and Gutchess, Jocelyn. *The Federal-State Employment Service: A Critique*. Baltimore: Johns Hopkins Press, 1970.

Smith, Abbot, E. *Colonists in Bondage*. Gloucester, Massachusetts: Peter Smith, 1965.

Smith, Adam. *An Inquiry into the Nature and Causes of the Wealth of Nations*. Edited by James E. Thorold. Clarenden: Oxford, 1880.

Spencer, Herbert. *Social Statics*. New York: Appleton, 1864.

Sumner, William G. *What the Social Classes Owe Each Other*. New Haven, Connecticut: Yale University Press, 1925.

Sussman, Marvin B., ed. *Sociology and Rehabilitation*. Washington, D.C.: American Sociological Association, 1966.

Thompson, James Westfall. *Feudal Germany*. Chicago: University of Chicago Press, 1928.

Todd, A.L. *Justice on Trial*. New York: McGraw-Hill, 1964.

Vollmer, Howard M., and Mills, Donald L., eds. *Professionalization*. Englewood Cliffs, New Jersey: Prentice-Hall, 1966.

Vroom, W. *Work and Motivation*. New York: Wiley, 1964.

Weedon, William. *Economic and Social History of New England, 1620-1789*. Vol. 1. 1890 reprint ed. New York: Hillary House, 1963.

White, George S. *Memoir of Samuel Slater and A History of the Rise and Progress of the Cotton Manufacture in England and America*. Philadelphia, Pennsylvania: n.p., 1836.

INDEX

Abbott, Grace, 19-22ff, 25, 45, 54
Abuses, by private employment agencies, 43-55ff; extent of, 53-55ff; types of, 44
Adams v. Tanner, 66, 67, 68, 79n
Advertising: by private employment agencies, 17; functions of false, 47; laws limiting, 46, 71, 80n; misleading, 44-47ff
Agency, private employment: early Anglo-American, 13-16ff; female domestic, 25-31ff; future of, 143-47ff; manual labor, 16-25ff; nature of business, 91-102ff; nineteenth century, 16-18ff; versus public employment agency, 73-78ff; white-collar, 33-38ff
Agency, public employment: early notion of, 13; establishment of, 57, 72-73ff; future of, 146; politics of, 74; versus private employment agency, 73-78ff
Agent, private employment, 1; forerunners of, 9-13ff. *See also* Job middleman, Locator
Anti-Defamation League, 51-52ff
Applicant, private employment agency: affect upon career of, 135-38ff; conditioning of, 110-13ff; agency criticism by, 129-31ff; dependency typology of, 114-15ff; immigrant, 20; sample of, 113-14ff; satisfaction with agency, 126-29ff; self-image of, 111, 118-22ff; suggestions for agency improvement, 131-35ff
Armstrong. *See People Ex rel Armstrong v. Warden*
Atwood, S. J., Mrs., 53

Becker, Howard S., 43
Blackstone, Sir William, 60
Blau, Peter M., 101
Blumberg, Abraham S., 99-100ff
Brandeis, Louis D. (dissenting opinions), 48, 67, 70
Brazee v. Michigan, 65-66ff
California Employment Agency Association, 103

Charities and the Commons, 71
Chusid, 144-45ff
Common law, 60. *See also* Constitutional law, Natural law
Conditioning: of applicants, 110-113ff, 114, 116; of counselors, 101-02ff; in reverse, 111, 112; universal approach, 112. *See also* Counseling
Constitutional law, 60, 61, 62, 64, 65. *See also* Common law, Natural law
Counseling, 75-76ff, 123-36ff. *See also* Conditioning
Counselor. *See* Private employment agent
Corvee, 9
Cowgill, Theodore T., 16, 39n, 45, 86, 87

Dicky. *See Ex Parte Dicky*
Discrimination, by private employment agencies, 50-53ff
Douglas, William O. (majority opinion), 70
Due process, 61; and regulation of business, 61, 62
Durkheim, Emile, 6n, 143

Employment and hiring, nature of, 4, 5
Ex Parte Dicky, 63, 64

Fee, for job middleman services, 15, 19, 20, 21, 26; state policies toward, 100n
Fee-splitting, 47-48; functions of, 47

Goffman, Erving, 110

Hall, Jerome, 59

Industrialization, 33; and distribution of occupations, 33, 34; and social legislation, 60, 61

Job middleman, 8; early Anglo-American, 13; medieval, 10. *See also* Private employment agent

Kahn, Herman, 143

158